Music
Mirror of the Arts
by Alan Rich

Project Improve
Irving School
9 Garden Place
Derby, Conn. 06418

Music
Mirror of the Arts
by Alan Rich

A Ridge Press Book

Frederick A. Praeger, Publishers · New York · Washington · London

*Dedicated to the memory
of Lucie Bigelow Rosen (1890-1968),
patroness of the arts, whose benevolence
mirrored the beauty she loved.*

*Editor-in-Chief: Jerry Mason
Editor: Adolph Suehsdorf
Project Editor: Moira Duggan
Project Art Director: Harry Brocke
Associate Editor: Barbara Hoffbeck
Art Associate: David Namias
Art Associate: Egbert Teague
Art Production: Doris Mullane
Art Research: Laurie Phillips
Art Research: Lucy Rosenfeld*

Preceding pages: Invitation to the Sideshow (La Parade), Georges Seurat

Contents

1. Music and the Visual Arts *page 6*

2. The Origins of Music *page 12*

3. Music as a Creation of the Intellect *page 32*

4. The Rise of the Renaissance *page 58*

5. Sixteenth Century: Time of Internationalism *page 78*

6. The Italian Baroque *page 104*

7. The Northern Baroque: Passion and Complexity *page 136*

8. The Rise of Romanticism *page 150*

9. Twilight of Classicism *page 172*

10. Flood Tide of Romanticism *page 196*

11. Since Wagner: The Tonal Heritage *page 228*

12. The Wagnerian Shadow *page 252*

13. Exploration and Reconciliation *page 270*

1. Music and

the Visual Arts

$\mathcal{E}$very work of art presents to the onlooker a long and subtle chain of reflections. First, its creator is mirrored—his state of mind at the time he brought the art work into being, as well as his general artistic outlook of which that state of mind is but an instant. And the artist himself mirrors his times. When we speak of his artistic outlook we suggest a series of ideas not formulated in isolation, but born out of the artist's reaction to the intellectual currents of his age. The artist may accept these currents, or purposefully choose to reject them. In either case the times have expression in his work.

Moreover, the influence of the times is felt by all the artists at work in any particular era. And this fact brings us to yet another depth in the mirror of art. For besides reflecting the artist and his times, the art works of a cultural era reflect each other, as well.

It is the purpose of this book to examine this last plane of artistic reflections, particularly how music mirrors the visual arts. This is not to suppose that exact analogies can be constructed between the arts, between this or that composition and a specific painting, sculpture, or edifice. Rather, it is to observe how broad principles have governed the working of creative artists in cultural eras. It attempts to intertwine the histories of music and the visual arts, where symbols and images, rather than words, are the means of communication.

The decision to select, from the broad spectrum of artistic creativity, only music, painting, sculpture, and architecture was not made arbitrarily. These are, after all, the nonverbal arts, the most abstract, the ones furthest removed from the principal bearers of information, i.e., words. It may be justifiably hazarded, therefore, that the relationships among the nonverbal arts is one of a special purity and subtlety. The relation between composer and poet and playwright is a somewhat more predictable one, no less fascinating, of course, for that. To compare music and the visual arts is, by comparison, a somewhat more dramatic contrast of opposites, merely from the fact that the one exists in time, while others have a continuing spatial existence.

In delineating these parallels, we will see, for example, how a Mozart symphony, composed late in the eighteenth century, embodies certain ideals found in the cultural currents that swept through Mozart's world at the time: a revival of interest in classical architecture, and the concomitant espousal of clean, balanced, symmetrical structure; a desire on the part of artists to evolve a manner of expression that is simple, immediate, and natural; a further desire to breathe into formal patterns a high degree of personal, fanciful utterance. The same holds true for many of the paintings produced at the same time, such as the early canvases of David. The artistic language of Mozart's time, in other words, is a special and recognizable blend of ideals. We can grasp these ideals when we listen with care and devotion to the works of Mozart and the other composers of his time, or when we look at the paintings of his contemporaries.

Going back further in history, it is striking to observe that at the same time composers in the early Renaissance began to show an awareness of tonality —of constructing a piece of music whose harmonies tended to seek out a certain goal, a certain distinct key—painters began to discover and formulate rules governing perspective. The two concepts—tonality and perspective—are closely linked.

Centuries later, in the early days of expressionism, the correspondence between the arts is again remarkable. Not only did Schoenberg, Kandinsky, Kokoschka, and their colleagues rub shoulders, they also dabbled in each other's media.

Today, in fact, in the final third of the twentieth century, we are going through a period of extremely close correspondences among the arts, quite possibly the closest in history. In reaction to the feeling of nihilism that came about at the close of World War II, there has come to many artists and composers a strong desire to make new beginnings, and to break down many of the old ideas about categories and divisions that existed, both among the arts and within a given medium of expression. Thanks to the huge improvements in communication—television, recording, superior means of reproducing works of art—we live our lives surrounded by an artistic jumble. Television itself, whatever its artistic status at the moment, both consumes and unites vast quantities of music and art material. As a consequence of this, at least in part, creators

Opening pages (from Kunsthistoriches Museum, Vienna): Order, design, and personal involvement —earmarks of composers no less than painters —are governing factors in Vermeer's L'Atelier, *created just before the time of Bach and motivated by a kindred spirit.*

9

are working in what has come to be known as "mixed media," in which the old notion of the integrity of one mode of expression has given way to the idea of a meaningful blend of many modes.

Thus, an art museum will bring in a group of avant-garde musicians to provide an "atmosphere" for the presentation of its latest exhibit of avant-garde paintings. Contemporary painters join with contemporary composers and playwrights to produce entertainments that appeal simultaneously to ear and eye (sometimes even to touch and smell!). The avant-garde composer John Cage records on tape the comings and goings and bits of conversation of people brought together at a party, and calls the result a musical composition. Other composers join forces with electrical engineers to produce musical "atmospheres" in which flashing and flickering lights and projections become an integral part of the experience. Obviously, there are going to have to be new names some day to describe these combinations of experiences, but the important thing is that while they represent close correspondence among the arts, they continue to accommodate that quality of the individual artist that no words can illuminate, no analogies explain—personal vision.

In thinking of the arts in historic terms, there are two great dangers to be faced. One is the mistaken notion that history in some way implies "evolution" from a lesser to a greater sophistication. The story of the arts is not the unfolding of a single line of progression. It tells itself rather in a series of curves, of stylistic ideals which rise to a point of development and then are subtly altered into new ideals. The new ideals need not, however, represent a higher point on an imagined evolutionary scale. An opera from the early seventeenth century by Monteverdi is not a primitive study for a music-drama from the nineteenth century by Wagner. It is a fully formed and exciting art work on its own, with its own integrity.

The other danger is the idea that a given era in cultural history has some innate purity, that it began from a hypothetical Point Zero and completely obliterated its past. Every age achieves a mixture of certain basic and timeless principles: the principle that we sometimes call "classic," which has to do

10

with controlled form and design, and the one which might be called by names like "Gothic," "baroque," or "romantic," and has to do with fantasy and freedom of expression. These "pure" concepts, meeting, mingling, and parting, provide a continuing dynamic in the story of the arts from the dawn of history to the present time.

But what of the "purity" of these concepts within the time of their currency? Must we confine ourselves to the architecture and painting of, say, Mozart's own time in order to illuminate our grasp of his music? Why can't we also observe Mozartian constructive principles in the clean lines of Bauhaus architecture from our own century?

These are valid questions, and the answer, of course, is that the analogies suggested here are based on general principles, not rigid likenesses. A Bauhaus building does have the clean lines of a Mozart symphony, but its general artistic language has none of the particular kind of graceful artifice that is also part of the eighteenth-century style. It represents a classicism that is mingled with other elements of its own time, as a classic structure of the eighteenth century is a formation of that period. The currents that inspired the Bauhaus classicism also produced in music a distinctive, twentieth-century classicism: the neo-classicism of Stravinsky, for example, or such sports as Prokofiev's *Classical* Symphony. In other words, no age represents any aesthetic principles in their pristine purity. It creates its own multiplicity of ideas out of the tangled skein of life at the time.

In a broad sense, there are artistic outlooks that leap across the centuries, that unite the gigantic power of a Michelangelo in the sixteenth century with that of a Beethoven in the nineteenth. But this force is something beyond the historian's obsession with labels and dates; it is the force of genius.

The final perfection of an art work, the last link in the chain of reflections, is the person whom the creator reaches with his art. This is the listener or the viewer, the person touched, repelled, exalted, bored, involved, annoyed . . . but in one way or another, moved. He is the reason why the arts exist and in a very real way, therefore, the clearest mirror of the arts.

2. The Origins

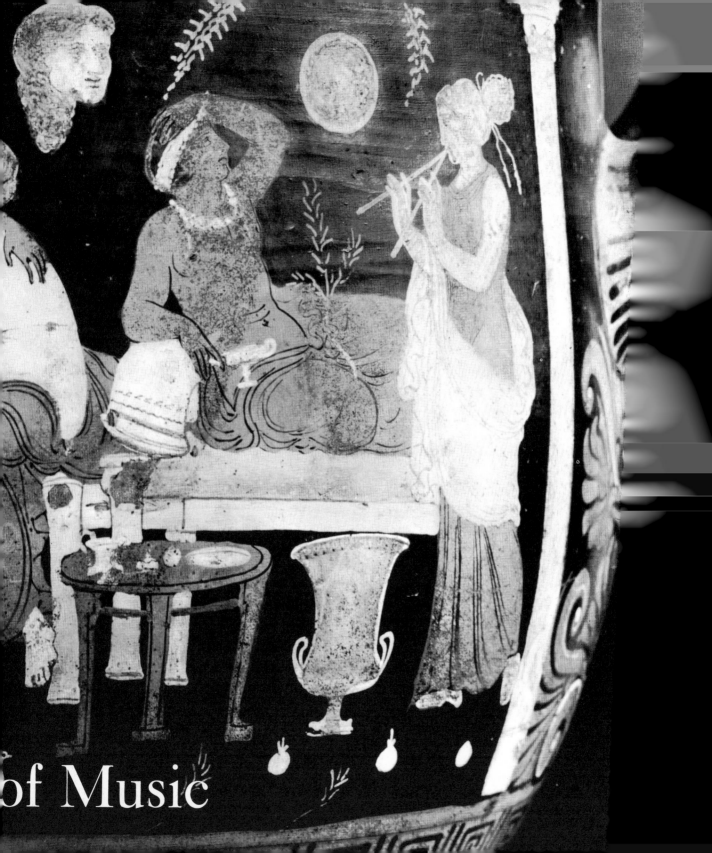

of Music

*W*alking along the beach one day, Mercury found a tortoise shell to which dried shreds of sinew still adhered, stretched from front to back and capable of producing a musical sound when plucked. He gave it to Apollo, who fashioned therefrom the lyre.

This is the Greek view of the origin of music, that it came from gods concerned with general wisdom and enlightenment. The Egyptians, likewise, ascribed the lyre to a god of wisdom, Thot; the Indian view credits Narada, goddess of learning, speech, and eloquence, lawgiver and astronomer.

We have very little firsthand knowledge of the music of the ancient world. It did not survive because very little of it was written down. It was an improvised art, governed by intricate rules regarding melody and rhythm, and its practitioners were expected to be able to create the proper song or dance for the proper occasion at the time the music was needed. Thus, while we possess an endless treasure of art works from the distant past—buildings, statues, jewelry, paintings, poems, plays, and philosophical writings—our understanding of music must be reconstructed from secondary sources such as treatises on music and pictorial representations of musicians.

Even so, we know a great deal. We know that music was an extremely important element of most advanced civilizations and that it played a crucial role in the life of every citizen. It increased the sense of mystery in religious ritual. It lent passion to the recitation of poetry and the enactment of drama. It stirred the souls of men in battle and brought grandeur to the ceremonies of government. It created in the home the proper atmosphere for contemplation and serenity.

Evidence of the role of music appears early. Paleolithic cave paintings show ritual dances, probably tied to puberty rites and animal sacrifices. Egyptian art from as early as 2680 B.C. shows singers, dancers, and instrumentalists. Paintings and sculptures from ancient Crete depict women in highly suggestive dance positions. The Oriental artistic heritage has numerous works in which assemblies of musicians and dancers appear.

Plato and Aristotle engage in lengthy discussions on the part music must play in an enlightened world. They reject certain kinds of melody as weakening to the intellect, preferring other types as more inspiring. Throughout the Orient, and especially in India, there is the same attempt to impart an ethical significance to certain musical patterns.

All this is tantalizing to contemplate, but the music itself no longer exists. Eleven short fragments of Greek music have been deciphered, at least approximately, but they are late, well after the death of Christ, and give no inkling of the richness of the musical repertory in the Periclean age. In the case of Oriental music we can consider ourselves closer to ancient sources, because these civilizations, isolated from the West until comparatively recent times and relatively self-contained, do show in their current musical styles a remarkable persistence of ancient tendencies.

Thus, the ethical values attached to Indian music can be observed today in the classical Indian music that is being popularized in the West by recordings and traveling artists. Indian music is luxuriant, rich in detail and ornamentation, and each composition is built around a melodic pattern (the *raga*) to which some inner meaning is attached. There are ragas for various times of day; ragas of contemplation and joy, of birth, rebirth, and death. It is an improvised music, as was that of the ancient Western world, and it seems to have changed little in sound and purpose throughout its existence.

Although Greek music is no longer extant, the concepts which shaped it, technically and philosophically, are both accessible and crucial. The very notes which make up our scales are the result of experiments with a stretched string done by the mathematician Pythagoras; from his findings also come our concepts of harmoniousness and dissonance. And even though our Western music pays little heed today to the Platonic ideal whereby certain melodic patterns weaken the intellect and others strengthen it, the underlying concept is still honored in a general way. The Platonic ideal, that music should serve to govern the intellect and lead the minds of men toward serenity and order, stands as one part of a duality which we will observe at work again and again in all the arts. Order, shapeliness, serenity—these are the elements of the

15

concept of *ethos*, the calmness of the soul, the wisdom of self-control. It expressed itself among the Greeks in the symmetry of the Parthenon, in the logical structure of their drama, in the heritage that has been referred to throughout the ages as *classical*.

The antithesis, the other member of the duality, is the concept of *pathos*—passion, suffering, and the accidents of destiny that give rise to the emotions. Ethos and pathos, among the Greeks and in every civilization since their time, tend to balance one another while operating antithetically. If ethos can be said to bring serenity, then pathos is the element of discontent, of movement or change. The ethos exemplified in the architectural designs of the Acropolis finds its antithesis in that timeless symbol of suffering from a Greece of not many years later, the Laocoön of the Hellenistic period; an equally striking example, the Dying Niobid, comes from the very time of Pericles and the building of the Parthenon.

Ethos and pathos—static order and dynamic momentum, repose and tension, harmony and dissonance—by whatever names we call these conflicting elements, they form the essence of art and were well understood by the Greeks. Even without having access to the music of the Greeks at the height of their civilization, it is reasonable to expect that it encompassed the same duality that we observe in the plastic arts of that age that have survived.

One thing we do know about this music. It consisted entirely of a single line of melody, perhaps supported now and then by an instrument. In this respect all ancient music, Eastern and Western, sophisticated or primitive, is alike. True, any line of melody implies a harmony, as we can easily tell by singing a familiar tune to ourselves, but until relatively modern times the harmonic sense in all music remained merely implicit. The devices of counterpoint and harmony, whereby several musical ideas proceed simultaneously and produce an effect through their interaction, belong entirely to the music of the Western world from the Middle Ages on. They developed, interestingly, at the same time when the fashion of regarding music as bearing some moral significance began to recede.

16

اغرب والصواب ان نزوجه بهاوشان ان مزنهم
في ذلك فاجابتهن اليه فعلوا الهاعرشا
واستنبدلوا با لجزن فرحاوبالمناجحة طربا
ولكثره غنابهن اخرجن حلبهن وفاخرثيابهن
وتزينن وسردنَ وصرن يغنين ويقلين يشوع
بن داودمثدلا لغم فرحا

*O*pposite: Seated man
with harp is
Cycladic sculpture of
c. 250 B.C.
Above: Pakistani stone
relief of musicians
and dancers, 1st
or 2nd century.
Left: Musicians of
11th century blow and
pluck instruments
in Oriental manuscript.

Among the Greeks, the Romans who inherited their traditions, and the peoples of the Orient, music in its purest state was something inspired by forces higher than mankind. As such, it was something simple and elemental: a melody, perhaps a rhythm. When compositional complexity entered music, many centuries later, it was the creation of man himself, confident at last of his own unfathomed creative powers.

*O*pposite: Durga (left), Indian goddess of fierceness and war, in 7th-century stone sculpture. Praxiteles' Hermes, (right) is one of the glories of Athens' "golden age." Below: Lyre appears again in Greek vase of c. 475-465 B.C.

MUSIC IN THE SERVICE OF ONE GOD

The Greeks and Romans embodied their gods in marble sculptures and clay figures. Oriental deities smile and dance in bronze and ivory. But the One God of the Hebrews commanded that He remain invisible, that there be no graven images to limit His omnipresence with human dimensions.

And so He was honored instead with music and poetry. His praises resounded in the Psalms and in the prayers and entreaties of home and temple.

The Psalms themselves give us many insights into the kind of music they inspired. There were instruments of all kinds, for Psalm 150 tells us to praise Him with timbrel and dance, with strings and pipe and sounding cymbals. Psalm 136 creates the unmistakable atmosphere of the service. The cantor intones his lines and after each the congregation responds: "For His mercy endureth forever."

We know far more. As with the Greeks and the Indians, the Hebrews organized their scales into set patterns, and each mode carried with it a strong ethical interpretation. There were specified modes for certain times of day and for certain elements in the worship. There were modes that were favored and others less highly regarded.

Much of this music has survived in diverse ways. Isolated Semitic tribes in the Near East still use a form of chanting that recalls unmistakably the things said by ancient writers about Hebrew music. Sephardic settlements in the western Mediterranean regions likewise preserve the ancient heritage they brought with them to Spain and North Africa. Wherever they have migrated, close-knit orthodox sects have clung tenaciously to their past. Today, in their

19

austere and unadorned places of worship, we may hear something close to what their ancestors heard.

It is a music of great and languorous beauty. The prevailing ideal is extensive and intricate improvisation. From a simple melodic pattern, unwritten but transmitted intact from generation to generation, the singer takes flight with elaborate, decorated coloratura, often breaking into falsetto and melodic swoops of astonishing difficulty. Like all ancient music, it is a single, unharmonized melodic line, but in its profuseness it constantly suggests a rich harmonic implication, passionate and exotic. Today's Jewish composers have been able to extract a rich source of inspiration from this musical tradition and to translate it into modern terms. Ernest Bloch's *Schelomo* transfers the ancient cantorial chant to the solo cello and brings the listener into the heart of the Jewish musical heritage.

THE MUSIC OF EARLY CHRISTIANITY

In the beginning, Christian worship differed little from that of the Jews. The first services were held in the same temples, and partook of the same music. The ideals that governed the place of music in the Christian ethic were also similar. "Speaking to yourselves in psalms and hymns and spiritual songs, singing and making melody in your heart to the Lord"—these words of Saint Paul in his Epistle to the Ephesians set forth the role of music in the Christian community.

As Christianity spread westward into Europe in the first millennium after Christ, its ritual—and particularly its relationship to the arts—underwent considerable change. At its source it remained close to the Jewish-Near Eastern ideal. Even there, however, it began to embrace ideas from outside the Jewish world. Throughout Christendom the visual arts joined with the arts of speech and song in the celebration of the One God.

From the heritage of ancient Byzantium, the metropolis of Asia Minor, it summoned to itself the fanciful and fantastic in the arts of fresco and mosaic. In this great city, later to become Constantinople and still later Istanbul, had

22

been united the ideals of ancient classicism and the Orient. The clarity and symmetry of classic art became blended together with the richly colored, curling designs of India and Persia, with their lavish use of gold inlay and the air of mystery that comes from figures elongated and mysterious, human and yet austere and remote from humanity. The Christians recognized the value of the visual arts in spreading their teachings; here was a way of reaching the masses of people who could not read, but who could immediately grasp a message in pictorial form.

And so the Eastern Christians developed a ritual harmonious with its Byzantine setting; vestments, incense, gesture, song, all combined to occupy and elevate the senses. One need only examine the miraculous adornments that have survived in the Hagia Sophia of Constantinople to experience the lavish panorama of worship in that basilica during the years it belonged to Christianity.

Further westward, however, the Christian ideals developed on a simpler level. Saint Augustine of Hippo writes in his Confessions of a virtual fear of

*P*receding spread: Furious battle between Greeks and Amazons is from frieze of Mausoleum at Halicarnassus, one of Seven Wonders of the World. Below: Despite destruction, Parthenon, most renowned unit of Athens' Acropolis, is still epitome of symmetry and proportion that give meaning to the word "classic."

the elaborate Eastern manner of singing the psalms. He wants a simpler chant, for he suspects the power of the singing voice to attract too much attention to its own brilliant effects and away from the words.

The aim of Christianity, wherever it spread, was to reach the people in the most direct manner possible. In Rome, which became the center of Western Christianity despite three bloody centuries of persecution, the first Christian churches incorporated the plan typical of Roman public buildings: a long central hall lined with classic pillars and narrow aisles on either side. This was the plan of the original Basilica of Saint Peter, for example, begun in 333 A.D. It may still be observed in many other great churches in Italy dating from the first six decades of the Christian era.

If early Christianity borrowed its architectural designs from its Roman hosts, the same may be said for its other art forms. Mindful of the Hebraic stricture against graven images, the early Christians at Rome were not very prolific in representing the body of faith through pictures and sculptures. But by the fourth century the bars seem to have loosened; Roman Christians began to decorate their churches and other meeting places with lavish designs illustrating familiar stories from the Bible, both Old and New Testaments. At first, these too were directly inspired by earlier Roman designs: classic-looking figures in classic poses, not very much different from the frescoes at Pompeii. One of the earliest representations of Jesus, taken from the sarcophagus of Junius Bassus, shows Him beardless and garbed entirely as if He were a classic god. As was the case with much early theology, Christ is represented more in His divinity than in His humanity.

To create a liturgical music repertory with a similar sense of continuity, the Roman Christians drew their psalm tunes not from the lavish and orna-mented Eastern repertory deplored by Augustine, but from the simpler and more tuneful songs of the people. What little we know of pre-Christian music on the Italian peninsula, in fact, is from the way these songs have been preserved within the church.

In 313 the Emperor Constantine granted Christians rights and protection,

*O*pposite: Hellenistic sculpture of Laocoön and sons punished by serpents for warning Trojans of wooden horse illustrates concept of "pathos" in Greek design. Above: Roman lady in wall painting plays cithara, ancestor of guitar.

25

and the growth of the church was assured. Now it became time to unify the churches of Europe so that God would be worshipped in like manner by all Christians, at least throughout the western half of the Christian world. Church leaders saw that in order to unify the liturgy, it would be necessary to unify its music.

The principal center for the organization of Christian music was not Rome, but Milan. There the Bishop Ambrose, friend and colleague of Augustine, at the end of the fourth century made the first attempt to compile a uniform collection of texts and songs and to write them down. A system of musical notation was devised, primitive by our present-day standards, but still serving to show the general direction and shape of melody. Small hooked symbols, known as *neumes*, were placed over the words on the parchment, and their position on the page indicated at least roughly how the melody was to be sung.

Ambrosian chant, some of which has persisted in the liturgy of the Cathedral of Milan, still bears some resemblance to the music of the East. Most of the melodies are simple, but there often are long coloratura passages that retain a definite Byzantine flavor. As in the Hebrew rites, there is often antiphonal singing, with the words of the cantor answered by the congregation.

As the church grew, permanent choruses of trained singers were maintained by the larger places of worship, and the body of liturgical music continued to develop. Two centuries after Ambrose's pioneering efforts in codifying the liturgy there was yet more work to be done. The culminating reform of Christian music was undertaken by Pope Gregory I, "the Great," during his reign of fourteen years (590-604). Despite the medieval legends, Gregory did not himself compose very much music (nor did Ambrose). His achievement was to call together the entire body of church chant, retaining what he felt to be fit music for its purpose, commissioning new music when necessary and producing a collection which could serve once and for all as the liturgy for the entire Christian year. With but few additions at later dates,

Gregorian chant alone served the Western church for nearly ten centuries, and it serves much of Catholicism today.

The ideals of Gregorian chant are both specific and timeless. They are the clearest example we have of the ancient attitude toward the relationship of words to music, and it is an attitude which is basic to the nature of music. The curve of the single line of music is inextricably linked with the shape of the Latin text it serves. It rises and falls with the sense and the sound of the words, breaking from simplicity to complexity as its text reaches its climactic thought. The melodies themselves have an innate sense of symmetry that relates clearly to the Greek ethos; an upward leap in the line, for example, is invariably balanced by a smooth descent.

The shape of the melodies themselves summons up a recollection of the Greek organization of scales and modes. Theoreticians of Gregory's own time had translated and commented on the nature of Greek musical theory, and the character of Gregory's collection of melodies shows little divergence from the classic ordering. There are eight principal modes, or scale-patterns, in Gregorian chant, and their names are bound to Greece: Dorian, Phrygian, Lydian, Aeolian, etc. Today's listener, trained in the two-mode (major and minor) system prevalent in most familiar music, may be startled at first by the richness and flexibility of Gregorian chant, and it is interesting that many composers in recent decades have sought to enrich their own music by a return to the old modal system. Brahms does it in the slow movement of his Fourth Symphony; Ralph Vaughan Williams' *Fantasia on a Theme by Tallis* is another modal work both modern and evocative of the past.

In a sense, Gregorian melodies have about them a certain austerity. We are quite sure that their rhythmic scheme was extremely free, bound to no pattern other than the flow of language. This sets them apart immediately from worldly music, especially music of the dance which must have regularly repeated rhythmic patterns. We are also reasonably sure that Gregorian chants were to be sung unaccompanied by instruments. Clearly the ideal was a disembodied music that would hover somewhere between heaven and earth,

27

*T*hree examples of flat, highly ornamented Byzantine style: *Madonna and Child Enthroned* (Italian, c. 1262), 8th-century St. Mark of pre-iconoclastic period, and mosaic of the Good Shepherd from mausoleum of Galla Placida, Ravenna.

*R*ight: Manuscript page from Gospels of St. Médard of Soissons (French, 9th century) is famous piece of Carolingian art. Opposite: Panel from Psalm 150 of Utrecht Psalter has figures at bottom pumping rudimentary pipe organ.

inspiring exaltation and awe in its listeners. That it does so still today is one of the miracles of music.

The term "Dark Ages," which has been variously applied to all or part of the first millennium of Christianity, is no longer regarded as fitting the time. In the sense that this was the time when Europe was beset by struggles and tensions, some of which rose out of the spread of the new faith, the term may be superficially appropriate. But the age also was one of artistic and spiritual achievement, and it ended in triumph. By the time of Charlemagne's death in 814, much of Europe was at peace and showing signs of a new flourishing of culture.

Artistically and philosophically, this millennium was, to be sure, rooted in the past. The obsession of Christianity was, to a large extent, to accommodate on some level the traditions of the people to whom it came. Thus, the persistent influence, especially in architectural outlines, of Greek and Byzantine aesthetics. Thus, the continuation of the Greek view that music is a moral force, along with the assimilation into the music itself of designs and concepts from the past. Thus, the permeation of Platonic ideals into the writings of the church fathers, Augustine among them. Thus, under Charlemagne, the revival of Greco-Roman styles in architecture and in painting, along with a great activity in translating the texts of classic Roman authors.

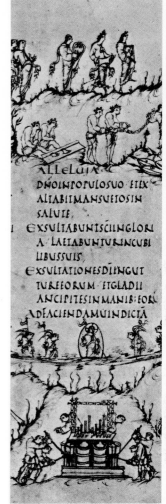

If the history of music had come to an end at this time, it would have been difficult to separate the styles common to Western music from those of highly developed civilizations in the Orient. Their substance consisted entirely of free melodic line. They shared also the richness of this form of composition, and each placed strong emphasis on improvisation. And they were rhythmically flexible, except where dancing was involved.

But this was only the beginning of the history of Western music. As the Carolingian era passed and the second millennium began, the paths of Oriental and Western music diverged dramatically. From 1000 A.D. to our own time the art of music has undergone a fantastic series of changes involving enormously complex additions to the basic, ancient structures and ideals.

31

3. Music as a Creation

of the Intellect

*A*rtistic currents, like all other currents, flow. Their changes of direction are never abrupt but are the results of stresses that have been at work for some time before the changes become sufficiently apparent to earn themselves a name.

The changes that swept through European art around 1000 A.D. grew directly out of attitudes that had been forming throughout the previous two centuries, certainly since the time of Charlemagne. We call this new creative period "Romanesque," implying that some sort of revival of Roman—or, at least, classical—ideals took place during this time. Actually, however, Christian aesthetic philosophy during the previous millennium had been to some degree directly influenced by Greco-Roman models, along with the richness and fantasy of Byzantine art.

And yet the new name was needed, because the eleventh century was the beginning of a new era, a time of tremendous increase in artistic activity in all fields. Architecturally, in particular, Europe gave the appearance of a garden that had suddenly begun to bloom. The new churches were grander in every way than those of the immediate past, larger and more lavishly ornamented. The older design for churches, the rectangular meeting-room with side aisles exemplified by the original Saint Peter's in Rome, gave way to a plan based on the Roman cross, with a long nave and transept to accommodate Christianity's increasing congregations.

Romanesque art is massive and imposing. This is true of its large buildings, and it is equally true of the designs that decorated these buildings. Elaborate carvings and sculptures, illuminating the important stories from the Scriptures, have a certain solidity even amid their flights of fancy. Fanciful they certainly are, with their processions of mythological beasts and monsters. But the wealth of detail built into these huge Romanesque monuments gave them a human quality that drew the worshipper even as he was awed by the enormity of the whole. Dwarfed and chastened by all that surrounded him as he entered the church, he was ready to receive the spiritual message.

One thing is clear. The explosion in the arts in the Romanesque era was the first stage in the ascendency of the human artist and the individual imagination. While the great bulk of building and decoration took place in the shadow of the church, the artistic contributions of the individual architects, sculptors, and painters were infused with a new degree of singularity.

This background is crucial to an understanding of musical developments at the time. Up to now, as we have seen, the important musical repertory of Christian Europe consisted of the collection of melodies assembled by Pope Gregory as the basis for the entire liturgy throughout every hour of every day of the church year—melody consisting of a single unison line to be chanted without accompaniment and, so far as we know, without such earthbound concepts as rhythmic pulse. Gregorian chant was held by church authorities as sacred and immutable, God-inspired, and not subject to human alteration.

But as God's buildings began to take on a new grandeur, the music designed to serve Him underwent a similar expansion. Sometime around 1000 a new concept—counterpoint—entered music. It was to establish from that time on the individuality of Western techniques. The first mention of counterpoint occurs in musical treatises dated within a decade of 1000. Evidently, therefore, the practice had begun sometime before—exactly when or where is not known. Somewhere, some time, it occurred to somebody that a given single line of chant could be enhanced by the addition of another newly composed line to be sung simultaneously with it.

This was no small matter, this addition by man to the divinely inspired musical substance. Whoever sanctioned the step must have been deeply concerned, morally as well as artistically. It is possible that the new contrapuntal line was regarded in the same light as much medieval scholarship: a kind of speculation, by means of a sort of marginal gloss, on the central text.

A more practical explanation, however, ties the birth of counterpoint to the other artistic currents of the time. Obviously, expansion of a musical line through the thickening of the texture reinforces the original sound. The new cathedrals—Mont-Saint-Michel, Canterbury, Westminster, and all the others—had a spatial vastness which, it may have been felt, should be filled

35

"*H*umanness" of Gothic apostles of Chartres (opposite) and Pythagoras (above) contrasts with static quality of late Romanesque apostle (above, left) and grotesquerie of hanging Judas carved on column capital of cathedral of Autun.

with a vaster sound. Like the church walls themselves, a new music had to be carved out with richer detail and greater massiveness than had previously existed. This theory can be borne out by the fact that most of the existing manuscripts of early counterpoint were found at some of the largest of the Romanesque cathedrals.

The nature of these first counterpoints was extremely simple. They followed the chant melody exactly but at an interval—usually the interval of a fifth (for example, from C to G) or a fourth (from C to F). Suppose we take a short tune: C-D-E-D-C. A contrapuntal melody a fifth higher would be G-A-B-A-G.

These intervals—the fourth and the fifth, along with the octave (C to C) —were the only ones considered harmonious at the time, and for a simple reason. Centuries before, Pythagoras had established a simple physical basis for harmony when he experimented with a string stretched between two fixed points. By dividing the string in determined ratios he obtained other notes. Dividing it in the ratio 2:1 gave him the octave; 3:2 provided the fifth, 4:3 the fourth. Other relationships—the third (C to E), which is the basis of our present harmonic system—involved much more complicated ratios and were therefore considered dissonances.

*G*rowing naturalism of late Romanesque art is also seen in carved wooden head of Christ and in luxuriant detail of Bayeux tapestry, which narrates William the Conqueror's invasion of England.

39

*P*receding pages:
Two views of Portal of
Smiling Virgin
at Amiens—flamboyant
Gothic at its peak.
Above: German King
Heinrich leads
orchestra in
15th-century Manesse
manuscript. Right:
15th-century German
oak carving of
Tree of Jesse.

42

This early counterpoint is known as *organum*, and the simplest form, described above, is *parallel organum*. If we play our simple melody with its organal line on the piano, or hear this kind of music sung, we are not so much aware of two lines of melody as we are of a single line with a wash of harmonic color. It is a fascinating, archaic color, however. Counterpoint had the effect of "spreading" the melody, a fact that lends support to the theory that musical space was expanded to fit greater architectural space.

From this simple beginning, the medieval composer could proceed to a somewhat more complicated next step. If there can be parallel lines, simple logic dictates that there can be non-parallel lines. In *oblique organum*, examples of which are found in eleventh-century manuscripts at Winchester Cathedral, the newly composed line has more melodic independence, moving at times in the opposite direction from the given line, still obeying the laws against dissonance, but running through the gamut of permissible intervals. A melody from Winchester begins A-A-G-A-C; the organal line above it also begins on A, then goes up to E, up again to G, back to E, and then to C. Thus, two melodies are combined in which the original curves downward and back, while the new one curves steeply upward and then back. Superimposed, they form a graceful and logical shape, and the ear hears each line as an independent musical thought.

From here on, the history of early counterpoint consists of the emergence of the new, freely composed melodic voice as an increasingly independent musical element. And not only one new voice, for many of the organa we have contain two or more of these new parts, all moving in the same time scale as the given Gregorian fragment, but interweaving back and forth in their melodic shape.

In the early twelfth century comes yet another step. Now the new voice is liberated rhythmically, as well as melodically, from the given melody. At the Abbey of Saint-Martial in southwestern France a new style emerges in which the given melody is sung very slowly in long, sustained tones. Above it the new voice moves, not in the note-against-note style of the earlier

43

organum, but in a quicker, more florid motion—many notes against one. What this does, in effect, is to attract the listener's attention far more to the new music, while the slow-moving chant recedes into the background. The composer himself, whoever he may be, begins to emerge and to assert his individuality.

Romanesque music is thus united with the other arts of the time in seeking to expand. As with the other arts, this expansion is not merely one of bulk or dimension, but of decorative detail in constantly increasing complexity. Just as one of the great art works of the period, the famous Bayeux tapestry of 1073-83, fills in its pictorial retelling of the Norman Conquest of England with a wealth of small decorative details, so does the new contrapuntal art fill in the outlines of the preëxisting "story," the given chant, with new contrivances. Gradually, as one can easily guess, the supporting framework of the new music, the original Gregorian melody, begins to lose its importance in the design; the ear is drawn to the complexity of the new inventions which surround it.

THE GOTHIC STYLE

Just as the term "Romanesque," describing the artistic currents that began around 1000, is somewhat misleading, so is the usual epithet for the ensuing currents. It seems likely that the term "Gothic" was coined by Renaissance scholars who sought to impute some taint of barbarism to the age preceding. The term takes its meaning from the style it encompasses.

The style originated in the Paris area around 1150 and spread through Europe within a century. By 1450 its domain had shrunk, although the Gothic manner continued to make itself felt in northern Europe for centuries thereafter. The keystone for the Gothic manner was the Abbey Church of Saint-Denis at Paris, completed in 1144.

This eloquent, grand structure departs from Romanesque ideals in several respects. While its proportions are large, there is a new feeling of lightness that contrasts markedly with the more massive Romanesque manner.

*P*age from Beaupré antiphonary of 1290, with musician at early organ. Square notes on four-line staff indicated pitch but not rhythm.

45

Its detail is more intricate. Its windows are larger, so that the interior is filled with dancing light, controlled and shaped by the designs in its stained glass.

Looking at Saint-Denis and other churches we see that Gothic art is both complex and delicate. Further, it breaks away from the abstract formalism of Romanesque sculptures in favor of a more personalized style, symbolic and distorted. The figures on the portico of the great Gothic cathedral at Chartres are tremendously elongated, as though straining toward heaven. Those on the façade of Notre Dame de Paris stand amid a lacy profusion of small designs, and the whole has been planned to assume a harmonious geometric consistency. One feels in such designs a persisting tendency toward formalism, as had marked the previous centuries, yet now tempered with a degree of fantasy and personal vision. The Gothic style is luxuriant and expressive.

It spread far beyond the confines of the church to permeate the life in cities and palaces. Palace walls were covered with fanciful, elaborate tapestries, wherein weavers captured the same intricacy, lightness of design, and symbolism that we find in the stones of the great cathedrals. This was the age of chivalry, of poetry extolling the virtues of sacred and secular love, of paintings telling of the unicorn, the mythical beast who could only be tamed by the attention of a pure maiden.

The earliest music of nonsacred character to have been preserved was that inspired by Gothic chivalric poetry. In France, troubadours and trouvères set their poetry to simple, elegant music consisting in most cases of a single melodic line, perhaps accompanied by a few notes strummed on a stringed instrument. These early secular melodies are far less complex and austere than the religious chants of the time, and suggest a rhythmic structure that would, of course, have been totally foreign to the liturgy.

Within the church, too, there was a turning to the new spirit of fantasy. In the twelfth and thirteenth centuries the students at many monasteries produced a repertory of liturgical dramas, familiar stories from the Bible with musical lines for the characters, to be acted on a simple stage or platform in a town square. These dramas, like the troubadour songs, were for the most

46

part set to a single, unharmonized melodic line; it would, of course, have been a cumbersome task to incorporate the new contrapuntal techniques in the telling of a story. But the dramas contained instrumental interludes, dances, and other elements of a decidedly nonliturgical nature.

Such innovations as these sacred sung dramas point up an important current underlying the Gothic revolution: the beginnings of a humanizing trend both in and out of the church. It is found in all the arts. We see it, for example, in the smiling "Golden Virgin" on the south portal of the cathedral at Amiens, or in the piercing grief of the faces in many depictions of the Crucifixion done at the time throughout Europe.

The passion for ornamentation and fantasy soon led to a passion for over-ornamentation. By the fourteenth century the Northern Gothic was tending to self-strangulation in the profusion and complexity of its designs. The cathedral at Amiens shows a decorative design which has been likened to tongues of flame, and from this we derive the term "flamboyant Gothic" to describe the manner at its most rampant.

As ornamentation in the arts grew mannered and excessive, music faced a new problem: how the various lines of counterpoint in a composition should be set down so that the performers could see how the notes of a given chant corresponded with the notes of its contrapuntal melody. In other words, there arose the problem of rhythm.

By the twelfth century, musical notation had made long strides from the primitive neumes of Bishop Ambrose. The great Italian theoretician Guido d'Arezzo devised the musical staff, so that the note symbols could be written in such a way as to show the exact pitch. Now, in the north of France, scholars found a system whereby the exact time duration of the notes could also be written down.

We cannot be entirely certain about the way music was actually sung in the twelfth and thirteenth centuries. Undoubtedly the florid upper parts of a composition were sung with a great deal of freedom and with some improvised embellishment. But the basic pulse of this music, it seems clear from the

*M*usicians from the pages of 14th-century Luttrell Psalter play small drums, portable organ, hurdy-gurdy, and bagpipe.

47

evidence, was conceived—as, by the way, it had been among the Greeks—in terms of the rhythmic modes of poetry: trochaic (EE-ny MEE-ny MY-nee MO), iambic (the STAG at EVE had DRUNK his FILL), and dactylic (THIS is the FOR-est pri-ME-val, the MUR-mur-ing PINES) being the most commonly used.

The church fathers had opposed strong rhythmic elements in sacred music as too worldly. Gregorian chant, its free flow determined by the cadence of speech, typified the ideal. But the new music demanded rhythmic organization, and the church could not resist. The personality that enters church art in the thirteenth century comes dancing into the church's music as well.

At Notre Dame de Paris there developed, just at the turn of the thirteenth century, a new school of composition of enormous resource and imagination. The great figures here, the first composers we can identify by name, are the monk Leoninus and his successor Perotinus. Together they produced a repertory of rhythmic organum that established Notre Dame in their time as the musical center of Christian Europe.

In the Notre Dame compositions an element of Gregorian chant still forms the basis. It appears in notes of tremendously long duration—the singers holding these notes were called *tenor* (Latin, *tenere*, to hold)—while one, two, or three upper parts move in rapid, rhythmicized melodic patterns of amazing complexity and of a light, dance-like nature. Some of the Notre Dame pieces lasted as long as fifteen minutes, and variety within them was obtained by occasional passages in the older note-against-note style (*clausulae*). The harmonic rules still apply. The basic intervals are still the "open" ones (fourth, fifth, and octave), but there are also passing dissonances on weak beats, providing a total sound far richer than anything heard before.

*V*aulted roof of choir at Amiens Cathedral creates illusion of almost limitless vertical space, an effect much sought after by Gothic architects.

In these Notre Dame pieces the singers taking the upper parts sang long vocalises on the words of the text of the original chant. The musical form which developed out of this style by the middle of the thirteenth century went one step further in introducing new texts as well as music. In the *motet*, the given chant was still taken by the tenor, but the upper parts received new

48

texts, usually commentaries on the basic text, but more verbose to fit the greater number of notes. Thus, as the tenor sings in honor of the Virgin Mary, the next-higher part may be singing some new words that speculate on the Blessed Virgin, and the topmost voice may have still a third text dealing in a more general way with chivalry or mother love. Often one or more of the upper parts may not even be in Latin, but in French or Anglo-Norman. Thus, in the motet, we have a structure which is polyphonic, polyrhythmic, polytextual, and polyglot. Flamboyant, indeed.

Other forms of composition also flourished, of which the most important is the *conductus*. Its name derives from the fact that it was sung at church festivities while the procession of priests was conducted to the high altar. Simpler by far than the organum and the motet, the conductus was in two, three, or four parts, but with a basic note-against-note movement in all parts. The most interesting feature of the conductus manuscripts was that in some of them all parts were newly composed; the Gregorian tenor does not always serve as foundation. Also noteworthy is that the plan of the pieces often included interludes to be played by instruments. From the scribes of the time we know that jugglers and dancers often joined the festivals at which the conductus was heard, so that conductus manuscripts are also of interest as our only source of the dance music of the mid-thirteenth century.

These dances are written out in a single melodic line or in two parts, but manuscripts and paintings of the time tell us that they were often accompanied by handclapping, drums and other percussion, and a wide variety of stringed instruments and winds. They are long and lovely works consisting of a number of regular musical phrases that alternate in a preordained sequence.

Much of the music described thus far permeated all of Europe, with France remaining the creative center. The one country which developed its own distinctive musical style was England. The successive invasions of the islands had left them rich in a varied, eclectic culture. The Celts, notably, had given to England a heritage of ornamentation that was energetic in design and richly colored. This spirit seems, centuries later, to have infused English music.

*C*rowded page of Sixth Trumpet, from "Four Horsemen" manuscript (Spain, 1220), was an attempt to create feeling of events in time and space, even as music of same era employed intricate counterpoint.

51

The strict continental attitude toward dissonance was viewed in a more liberal light by the English. The interval of the third, forbidden because of its "complex" Pythagorean ratio, had been accepted in England by 1200. From its beginnings, English polyphony is noted for the rich blending of its parts and the mellifluous sonority that comes from the use of thirds. It possesses a warmer beauty quite removed from the archaic "open" quality of the Notre Dame pieces.

The most famous piece of English music to survive from this time is not a religious work at all (although it seems to have been preserved in a religious manuscript), but the song *Sumer is icumen in*. This piece has always proved something of an embarrassment to historians, since it is about a century before its time in terms of style. It has been dated at about 1240.

The song is the earliest surviving example of a *canon*, a polyphonic work in which the voices enter one by one, each singing the same melody but at a different time. (The familiar *Frère Jacques* is another example of a canon.) Four voices engage in this canon, while two more lower voices have another, slower-moving canon of their own; in other words, a six-part composition. Actually, there are only two basic harmonies for the whole piece, so that the combinations work out very smoothly. This does not alter the fact, however, that this amazing and lovely work is composed in a manner that did not become important in the rest of Europe until late in the fourteenth century.

THE "NEW ART" OF THE FOURTEENTH CENTURY

It is a delicate matter to speak of evolution in art. Every era has its standards, its ideals, and its techniques. Nevertheless, there is a line which can be followed in tracing the history of the arts into the fourteenth century, and that line consists of a growing tendency toward personal expressiveness. There comes a subtle change in the concept of beauty, a turning away from mystery and inscrutability and toward simplicity. We saw its beginnings in the thirteenth century, notably in the sculptor's art. Now, at the dawn of a new century, it comes to pervade music as well.

A new doctrine was formulated in music around 1325, defined by a musician-theologian, Philippe de Vitry, and supported in writings by many of his students. A new music is proclaimed, to be known simply as *Ars Nova* (The New Art). Under this concept a new liberalism came into musical style. The interval of the third, already in use in England, was now to be permitted generally as a consonance. Strictures about rhythm were also loosened, permitting a more flowing, dance-like pace.

This doctrine is in essence a recognition of the inevitable on the part of the official. By the beginning of the fourteenth century ecclesiastical power was threatened by rising secular power in the cities and states of Europe. The Papacy had moved to Avignon from Rome in 1305 and ruled there for seven decades. The church, no longer in a position to ignore forces outside it, made its own pact with the world, bringing tunes and pretty, bright pictures from the profane world into its own sacred domain.

The New Art was not universally welcomed. There were still conservatives who deplored the "discords" of the new style, and in 1324 Pope John XXII issued an edict from Avignon decrying the new secularization of music and outlining punishments for those who practiced it. This edict did not dissuade composers from writing music in the new style. It merely turned them away from writing church music. For the first time we find the growth of a true musical art as an adjunct to secular society.

The principal exponent of the New Art was the French poet, soldier, statesman, and composer, Guillaume de Machaut. In a sense, Machaut's music stands as the purest translation of the ideals of the Gothic in art. It is a fanciful, highly ornamented style which makes great demands on the virtuosity of its performers. It is full of symbolic elements, little constructive "secrets" which are clearly meant to be hidden within the musical texture. And Machaut's large-scale musical designs show a control over shape that reflects quite obviously the strong Gothic tendency toward geometric structure.

He worked toward a single ideal: beauty in the life of the thinking man. The beauty he found was in the world around him: in nature, in love, and

Goddess Music sits holding portable organ while disciples play a variety of stringed and percussion instruments common in 14th century.

55

in the enjoyment of life's pleasures. Somehow, whether in or out of the church, he managed to translate all this into a kind of human godliness that rebuked and challenged the older, austere concept of godliness.

Machaut was, naturally, trained within the church, but he soon left it to lead fully the life of the world. His music partakes to some degree of the sacred forms of the previous century. He used the old polyphonic motet, with its slow-moving lower voice and its more ornate upper parts, as the model for his vocal pieces. But all of the parts were newly composed; there was no reliance on Gregorian chant to provide the lower melody. His models were old, but his style was new. The upper parts flow with a grace and an aesthetic logic that earlier and stricter principles preclude. The "new" harmony gives his music a feeling of resonance far removed from the "open" fourths and fifths of the earlier style.

We also encounter in Machaut's vocal pieces a new and sophisticated attitude toward musical form. Most of his pieces are worked out along the constructive principles that govern the poetry itself: repeating refrains, alternation of verses, unity, and contrast. In some of them there is a long rhythmic pattern in one or another of the inner parts which constantly repeats. This is one of his interesting "secret" devices. The pattern (called an *isorhythm*) is much too long for the ear to grasp, but it is there to support the structure of the work as the skeleton of a building supports its masonry. One of Machaut's most famous works is set out as a canon, except that one part is sung backwards in relationship to the others. The text of this piece explains its structure: *Ma fin est mon commencement* (My end is my beginning).

This kind of "inaudible order" which we often encounter in Machaut's music is probably tied to the symbolism of earlier theology. In any case, it is a principle that often recurs in the history of compositional techniques. It is interesting that the great rediscovery and revival of Machaut in Europe around 1910 occurred just before Arnold Schoenberg's formulation of the twelve-tone principles, which also depend to a large extent on certain inaudible structural devices.

56

Machaut's one important church composition is a setting of the text of the Mass, composed possibly about 1330, but more likely later on. It is important historically as the first polyphonic setting of the Mass text that can be ascribed to a single composer. It is important also because of its remarkable beauty, achieved and never obscured by its tremendous complexity. The work stands as the culmination of the sacred Gothic style: intricate, symbolic, austere in atmosphere, and deeply spiritual.

Complexity in music did not reach its height with Machaut. It grew even more pronounced toward the end of the century when for a brief period composers attempted pieces of a literally descriptive nature. The idea of "program music" was still a concept for the future, but the French *chace* and the Italian *caccia* (both meaning "hunt") were interesting antecedents of it. In them, two or more voices enter in canon, and the lines they have to sing are melodically shaped to imitate the sounds of a hunt: the barking of dogs and the whooping of the hunting horns. Of course, the very idea of a canon, with its voices "chasing" each other in musical imitation, suggests the hunt, but the addition of these contrapuntal evocations of dogs and horns adds a vivid pictorial touch.

Clearly, the composer at the end of the Middle Ages, along with the writer and the painter, is beginning to react with an awareness of the world around him. His predecessors found inspiration from more abstract, mystical sources, and expressed this inspiration in an art that was austere, purposefully symbolic, somewhat infused by awe. Now, at the dawn of the Renaissance, art begins to concentrate on human proportions, and to reproduce things as seen by the human eye and heard by the human ear. Art, in other words, has begun to mirror life.

Those words are usually applied to the prevailing spirit of the Renaissance, the era marked by man's growing awareness of himself in the world. It is clear, however, that the spirit of the Renaissance did not suddenly burst upon the world. By the end of the fourteenth century, the movement toward that ideal had already become firmly entrenched in the artistic language.

4. The Rise of

the Renaissance

Northern Europe was the birthplace of Gothic style, and there it held sway the longest. In the south—which is to say in Italy, since this was the major artistic antipode to France and England—its hold was less dominant, and by the middle of the fourteenth century it was swept aside by a new wave of thought currents.

Out of a mingling of several elements—the richness of the northern Gothic, the passion characteristic of Byzantine art, and, perhaps, the nature of the Italian temperament itself—there emerged a style of artistic expression that held a great deal more of immediacy and of emotional communication than was the case with the geometrically oriented Northern designs. An example of the latter can be seen in the thirteenth century altar panels of the Florentine Cimabue, whose gold backgrounds and sense of austerity link him clearly to Byzantine models. A few decades later Duccio of Siena takes Cimabue's designs and, in a sense, "thaws" them to provide paintings in which we can sense more palpably the presence of the human form. Duccio's figures are three-dimensional. His Madonna's garments hang naturally (with an intricacy of design that bespeaks the Gothic influence) and his faces reflect some kind of involvement in dramatic situations.

How define humanism? Simply put, it is that approach in art and philosophy which regards man as the center of things, and life on earth of an importance at least equal to life in the hereafter. Medieval theology tended to regard earthly life as merely a preparation for life after death, and this attitude can easily be seen as a prime mover in artistic currents through the Gothic era: the mystery, the symbolism, the distortions and elongations in both architecture and decoration, the proportions designed to produce a sense of awe. In music, the complexity of French and English medieval forms like the motet, the involved inner construction in Machaut's Mass, the disembodied quality of Gregorian chant—all these elements put it beyond the understanding of a large audience, making it—if only in that sense—antihumanist.

Now, at the beginning of the fourteenth century in Italy, there comes a change in artistic attitudes. We see it in the suppleness and naturalness of

Duccio's paintings and in the warm charm of other painters, like Sassetta. We find it, too, in the poetry and prose of the great humanist poet of the time, Francesco Petrarch, who sings of the beauties of nature and of the sorrows and greatness of man upon the earth. In the century before Petrarch, there are the beginnings of Italian humanism in the exalted visions of Francis of Assisi and, shortly after Francis, in the tormented visions of Dante. Now the movement burst out in full force.

Without doubt the most vital force in early humanistic art was Giotto, a Florentine and probably a student of Cimabue. In Giotto's frescoes, scattered throughout the Italian peninsula and most of them marvelously preserved, we find the humanist spirit vitally on its own, striking out from Byzantine and Gothic antecedents. Giotto's figures show an even stronger trend toward naturalism, but the most striking feature of his work is its simplicity and emotional directness. His backgrounds, as well as his principal subjects, are naturalistic, even when his skies are filled with hovering angels. There is great tenderness in his faces. One senses, as seldom before in painting, the possibility of actual conversation taking place between characters. Everything in his manner points to the artist as a participant; as with all supreme creative spirits after his time, he is concerned with creating not merely symbols or proto-photographs, but interpretations.

As these humanistic ideals continued through the fourteenth century, painters became more assured in dealing with human forms and motions and naturalistic settings. We see this increasing naturalism, for example, in the intricate nature studies in the frescoes of Lorenzetti. And we feel especially in the works of Lorenzo Masaccio, early in the fifteenth century, an outburst of passion, of suffering, of a willingness even to forgo formalism when it might interfere with a powerful depiction. Drama infuses Masaccio's work. One can almost hear the lamentations as Adam and Eve are driven from Eden. One can relate his Madonnas to the women he observed on the streets of Florence.

Fourteenth-century developments in music centered around the first major Italian composer, the blind Florentine organist, Francesco Landino, who

Opening pages: "Noli me tangere," fresco for life of Christ by Giotto in Scrovegni Chapel in Padua. Giotto's humanistic painting presaged rise of Renaissance, although dating from early 14th century.

61

62

translated into simple, shapely musical forms the growing awareness of beauty that his sighted colleagues were able to see around them. Landino's short secular songs have none of the inner complexity that typify the works of his contemporary, Machaut. They are contrapuntal, usually for two or three voices, and the lines are fluent and rhythmically simple. He delights in a rich interplay of sensuous harmony, using sounds as much for their pure color value as for any structural reasons. Melody, supported on the simplest harmony, is his primary means of communication.

It is beautiful music and it strikes us so today, perhaps more than does the elegant, elaborate, but austere music of the North. It is, like the art of its time, clearly prophetic of the coming explosion of individual creativity. Landino's dates place him somewhat later in the fourteenth century than Petrarch and Giotto, but the community of outlook among them is inescapable.

Harmoniousness, balance, simplicity, and grace—these were the attributes of Landino's music and, judging from contemporary tributes, it was immensely popular throughout Italy. Strange, then, that after this sudden outflowering of Italian musical activity the ensuing century is almost totally barren. What activity there was consisted largely of composers from the North visiting Italy and creating pieces with Northern complexity set to Italian texts. The true native musical art consisted entirely of a simple, charming repertory of songs usually set for two or more voices but with even less contrapuntal activity than we find in Landino. Even so, as we will later observe, these graceful, dance-like pieces attracted the attention of visiting composers and worked themselves deeply into their consciousness.

It must be said, then, that the crucial century in which the Italian Renaissance was actually shaped, the fifteenth, saw greater creativity in the visual arts than in the field of music.

THE NORTHERN STYLE

Philip the Good (1396-1467), Duke of Burgundy, was a lover of luxury, art, and music. His dukedom included most of northeastern France, Flanders, and

*O*pposite: Contrasting portraits of Virgin and Child are by contemporaries of Giotto. Cimabue work (left) has stiff formality of earlier styles; Duccio's is suffused with greater naturalism. Above: Masaccio's expulsion of Adam and Eve from Eden, painted a century later, erupts with passion.

63

the Low Countries, and under his benevolent patronage there flourished one of history's great assemblages of artistic creators. To it belonged such men as the composers Guillaume Dufay and Gilles Binchois, the painter Jan Van Eyck and possibly his brother Hubert.

To the court of Burgundy came also, either in person or through manuscripts, the towering English composer John Dunstable. In Dunstable's music we find expressed on the highest plane the ideals we noted previously in English music: the rich, sonorous harmonies, attractive and symmetrical melodic lines, and a special concern for the union of words and music. He wrote music that follows, in its general outlines, some of the intricate polyphonic forms of fourteenth-century French composers like Machaut. But there is, in Dunstable's works, a new feeling for simplicity and beauty that points in a direction entirely different from the aloof complexity of Machaut.

The old idea of the motet, in which a line taken from Gregorian chant supports several newly composed and faster-moving melodic lines, was used by Dunstable with a new degree of freedom. Into a contrapuntal setting of a Mass text, Dunstable wove a melodic line from a preëxisting composition: a chant, or even a popular tune. This *cantus firmus* ("firm" chant in the sense of "given" or "unchanged") becomes incorporated into the texture and lends structural support. It moves, not entirely in slow notes, but with rhythmic flexibility. It is there to be heard as an equal with the other parts. In other words, the older system of polyphony loses its rigidity with Dunstable and takes on a more natural and varied flow.

This freedom allowed Dunstable another kind of style. No longer working from the necessity to contrast fast-moving upper lines with a slower tenor, he could move all voices of a three- or four-part composition at the same speed, thus giving his music the effect of a series of chords. They were not chords in the way that our simple church hymns are played and sung today. Each of the voices was laid down as a separate melodic idea. But the effect is of a slow-moving wash of harmony; the attention is focused upon beauty of sound heard as a single melody.

64

This music had a pronounced influence on the Burgundian composers. It awoke them to a sense of beauty expressed in the simplest terms. The early works of Dufay, as of Dunstable, have some of the mannered complexity of the late Gothic style. Later, as he evidently came to know the music of Dunstable, there is a marked change. He begins to react toward the power of harmony to "pull" the ear toward a point of reference—what we would call today a *key* or a *tonality*. In his music we can truly feel, for the first time, the elements we accept in the concert music most familiar to us: harmonic regularity, a melody which has a recognizably lyric shape, clear and symmetrical rhythms.

What we are talking about here is the musical counterpart of a new spirit that came also into painting. When we say that a musical composition begins to show harmonic "pull," we are establishing the musical equivalent of the horizon in painting. When a piece of music is in a certain key—C major, say—we mean that melody and harmony tend toward C as a point of reference.

Strictly speaking, Burgundian and Flemish painting of the early fifteenth century still holds to certain Gothic principles. The break is not so clear as it was, even a century before, in Italy. Even so, amid the continued complexity, the symbolism, and a certain lingering worship of detail for its own sake, a new spirit can be discerned. It comes into full realization in the works of the brothers Hubert and Jan Van Eyck, who worked in the orbit of the Burgundian court for a time during Dufay's years there. Within the Gothic tradition, the brothers accomplished a degree of humanness, if not exactly humanism, that constitutes a marked break with the mysticism of earlier Gothic art.

To accomplish this they perfected a new medium, a paint made from oils rather than the water and egg yolk of their predecessors. Painting with oils enabled them to build up layers of color, bringing depth, iridescence, and light into their work. From this basic beginning they were free to experiment with perspective and proportion. There is richness, warmth, and joy in their great altarpiece, *Adoration of the Mystic Lamb*, a spirit never before encountered in Northern painting, certainly not in religious painting. But perhaps even more remarkable is Jan's *Portrait of Jan Arnolfini and His Wife*,

65

*A*bove: Detail of angel playing lute, from *Mary, Queen of Heaven*, is by Master of the St. Lucy Legend, c. 1480. Opposite: Jan Van Eyck's painting of Giovanni Arnolfini and his bride is cornerstone work of Northern Renaissance.

with its highly individual subjects, the feeling that life is going on outside the quiet room, the mirror on the back wall that even shows someone about to come into the room, and the little dog in front that is tensed to bark at the intruder.

Music and painting as living beauty, natural and real: this is the spirit of the new age as it took form in Philip's dukedom. What is extremely important is that it took place on both a religious and a secular level. Dufay's music consists of many large-scale religious compositions, along with a number of polyphonic songs about love, drinking, and the outdoors. The Van Eycks painted altarpieces and Madonnas, but also did portraits. Whether the works are sacred or profane, there is no break or change in the artist's style.

The crossover between the things of God and those of Caesar worked toward a mutual enrichment. One of Dufay's most beautiful Masses is built around a popular song, *Se la face ay pale* (If my face is pale, the cause is love), which occurs as a cantus firmus in all sections. Another tune, *L'homme armé* (The armèd man), occurs in literally hundreds of fifteenth-century Burgundian Masses.

The setting of the Mass was the major musical form of the entire Renaissance, occupying the place among composers that the symphony did in the eighteenth and nineteenth centuries. The Roman Mass is composed of two elements: the *ordinary*, which is the fixed text used throughout the year, and the *proper*, which changes according to the day. A Mass-setting is a setting of the ordinary, which is in five main sections: Kyrie, Gloria, Credo, Sanctus (with Benedictus), and Agnus Dei. As instituted by Dunstable and carried forward in the fifteenth century, a Mass is a unified musical form, and the unity is provided by the cantus firmus, which recurs in one of the inner voices in all movements and is surrounded by free counterpoint. Occasionally this free material may also recur from section to section, and quite often its melodic shape may be determined by the melody of the cantus.

Dufay traveled widely in his late years and his Masses occur in manuscripts all over Europe. His mature works in this form, along with his colorful,

66

Virgin and St. John by van der Weyden (right) and Memling's *Presentation in the Temple* (opposite) also demonstrate emergence of personal, expressive style among 15th-century Flemish painters

charming songs, belong among the richest masterpieces of his or any time.

The ensuing generation of painters and composers saw men in both fields acquiring still greater assurance. It is true in almost any creative era that the beginnings are in simplicity and the growth is in complexity. The Northern mind—rational, scientific, and tidy—seems particularly apt for carrying out this axiom.

Rogier van der Weyden was one painter of the generation following the Van Eycks who continued the movement toward naturalism. This he accomplishes through a wealth of small details astonishingly attuned toward producing a single, telling emotional effect. The intensely passionate expressions of his faces are in the tradition of late Gothic works. Indeed, there is a distinct relationship between his paintings and some of the sculptures we find from the late fourteenth century. But his use of colors, and especially the continuation of the Van Eyck brothers' experiments in perspective, gives his

work a naturalness, a communication, that seem to transcend the Gothic ideal to some extent and to push toward the same immediacy that characterized Italian art works of the early fifteenth century.

Still, van der Weyden's work—in its insistence on symbolic representation, in the fact that his figures seem to be sculpted onto a flat surface rather than infused with deep humanness—keeps some of the aloofness of his Gothic past. So, indeed, do many of the paintings of Northern artists up into the sixteenth century: the symbolic conceptions of Memling, the emotional depth

*G*rotesque fantasies of Hieronymus Bosch—here musical— are in detail from *The End of the World.* Opposite: Brueghel's *Wedding Dance* shows Renaissance artist turning attention to mundane world.

70

of van der Goes' characterizations, the metaphorical fantasies of Hieronymus Bosch. The one aspect of these men's work that continues to develop in the direction of naturalness is that, among the crowded details, the multitudes attendant upon the depicted events, one sees the faces of highly individual, even unbeautiful people. Northern artists looked inside their own consciousness for their visionary subject matter, but looked to the man of the town, or of the fields, for their models. The culmination of this attitude was, of course, the remarkable series of folk studies by the last of the truly Gothic painters

*L*ady at left holds round-backed lute, a favorite instrument in 15th and 16th centuries. Detail is from painting by Cosmè Tura and Francesco Cossa.

of the North, Pieter Brueghel, who somehow effected a convincing mingling of the artificial stylization of fourteenth-century tapestry and book designs with the authentic sights of the countryside around him.

What characterizes Northern painting of the fifteenth century as a lingering Gothicism is the preoccupation with detail and fantastic patterns of the most intricate sort, the kind of approach to creation that signalized the very birth of the Gothic style in the twelfth century. And this same complexity, mingling to be sure with a growing feeling for euphony and approachable beauty, characterized the music in the generations of Flemish composers following Dufay.

In the works of Jan Ockeghem and his pupil Jacob Obrecht, both of whom died around 1500, we sense an outgrowth of some of Dufay's techniques. For one thing, the free intertwining of counterpoint develops now into a systematic kind of imitation, where each voice in turn enters with the same melody. We have encountered this before in the English *Sumer* canon and in some of Machaut's pieces. Dufay used certain techniques of this order, so that successive voices would imitate at least the beginning of a line.

Now, however, the device was carried forward in a far stricter manner so that an entire line is imitated by four or five parts entering in turn. Furthermore, Ockeghem and Obrecht delighted in all sorts of interesting mathematical variants of the imitative technique. A work might be planned something like this: a voice begins with a melody, another enters with the same melody but in a slower or faster motion, then another takes the same melody but upside down or backwards. Often the composer would write out only a single line, leaving the performer to puzzle out the other parts. Some of the Flemish "puzzle-canons" are still unsolved.

And yet, for all this antinatural complexity, the Masses of Ockeghem and Obrecht have freshness, clarity, and a deep expressive quality. The constructive devices are the composer's own secrets. Like those of the Gothic fourteenth century, they are not meant to be heard. What is heard instead is an orderly, euphonious progression of sound, falling into natural and simple patterns.

72

THE FUSION OF NORTH AND SOUTH

By the end of the fifteenth century, two great poles of artistic thought and style may be discerned. In the North, where Gothic tendencies persisted, art forms retained a certain austerity combined with a delight in speculation that was philosophical in its preoccupation with inner meanings, and scientific in its predilection for mathematical intricacy and the solving of "puzzles." This set of artistic aims mainly influenced painting and music, although it also had a marked effect on architecture and sculpture. It claimed adherents not only in the Low Countries, but also in Germany, France, England, and Spain.

The other great artistic pole was in Italy, where, as early as the fourteenth century, a new approach to life had begun to be formulated. It was recognized by those who lived under it and described everywhere as a Renaissance, a rebirth. Its motivating principles were founded in a restudy and re-evaluation of the classical heritage of Greece and Rome, so that both the artistic and philosophical principles of those ancient cultures might be reconciled with Christian thought. In that reconciliation, man the creator found himself endowed with far more power than he had been hitherto conscious of possessing.

The new humanism, the new importance of man, manifested itself in the arts in a warmth, a serenity, an emotion, a sense of smiling naturalness. Filippo Brunelleschi, in a single stroke, swept away Gothic architectural design when he created the Duomo of Florence, its vertical space capped by a serene, seemingly suspended dome, and its shape punctuated by Roman columns and arches. Brunelleschi's design was not merely a slavish imitation of old models; it was a seeking to translate classic form and space into the language of his own century.

Brunelleschi's Duomo may be said to epitomize the Greek ethos, the serenity of formalism and symmetry. Donatello, on the other hand, created a repertory of sculptures that epitomized pathos, their powerful, irregular designs fraught with passion.

And there was Leonardo da Vinci, who perhaps best epitomizes the spirit of the Renaissance. His inquiring mind re-expressed the whole range of intellectual exploration of the Periclean age, while also exploring the outer

74

limits of newly acquired techniques and ideals in painting, architecture, and sculpture. In Leonardo's paintings we find, unmistakably expressed, a vivid range of emotion and reaction: delight, suffering, wisdom, calm, tension, even inscrutability.

The Italian manner was to cast its influence throughout Europe, and eventually to dispel the lingering Gothicism of the North. Albrecht Dürer, a Northern painter in his luxuriant, meticulous, and intricate detail (and in this way united to the Flemish composers of the late fifteenth century), reacted markedly to Italian influences after his visits south, and effected in his finest works

*O*pposite: Brass ensembles ring out in della Robbia relief (top). Below: Classic grandeur of Roman dome was revived by Brunelleschi for Duomo in Florence. In contrast, Donatello's Abraham breathes the spirit of pathos. Left: Italian lyricism pervades da Vinci grouping of Virgin and Child with St. Anne and infant Baptist.

a true synthesis of the two outlooks. Serenity, order, and a freedom in the use of color are the Italian contributions to his style.

Musically, the fusion is epitomized in the works of the composer whom historians come more and more to proclaim the supreme composer of the Renaissance, Josquin des Prés. And, as we bring this study of the fifteenth century to its closing years, it is the music of Josquin that serves to bind together two divergent cultural streams.

Josquin was a native of Flanders, born there about 1450. In his early years he was clearly allied with his countrymen Ockeghem and Obrecht, working as they did in a complex style involving continuous imitation. In this style he wrote a superb repertory that includes religious compositions and songs. His funeral song (*Déploration*) on the death of Ockeghem, with its throbbing vocal writing, its long, descending melodic lines colored by poignant harmonies, stands as one of the most moving compositions of any age.

By 1470 we locate Josquin in Italy, attached for a time to the court at Ferrara, and possibly also a visitor to the great intellectual and artistic gathering at the Florentine court of Lorenzo de Medici. Here he became imbued with the sunny, simple, lighthearted Italian style, and it had a remarkable effect on his own music. His compositions become simpler, more open, more given to the sheer beauty of sound. Josquin composed a number of highly artistic songs in the Italian manner, and the Italian style even permeated his church music. In one of his most famous works, a long setting of the hymn *Ave Maria*, there are frequent places where he abandons the polyphonic style and sets a whole section as a progression of chords. The effect of this variety within its context is electrifying.

More than any composer before him, Josquin understood the importance of variety and contrast in organizing a large-scale composition. In his simple, open textures, free to a large extent of the intricacies of his Flemish compatriots, we sense a real emphasis on a melody supported by secondary voices which provide harmony. In these two respects alone, Josquin can be considered the first "modern" composer.

76

In other respects, too. In his compositions there is an extraordinary care in the setting of key words. He uses the power of harmony to suggest passion. He indulges in word painting. A poignant word will evoke a particularly dark harmony, a lighthearted word will perhaps take wing in a short vocal cadenza. His compositions have a quality that is entirely new in music: they are vivid, in the same way the works of later great dramatic composers—Monteverdi, Bach, Mozart, Verdi—are vivid.

Josquin's journeys took him back and forth between Flanders and Italy, and also to France, where the creative arts had been burdened in the fifteenth century by the yoke of prolonged civil strife. In all way stations on his journey, however, the liberal outlay of his own genius set a standard. He wrote the best Flemish, French, and Italian music of his time, and he was recognized for so doing. He possessed in music that quality which, above all, defines the spirit of the Renaissance—the quality of imagination.

*N*orthern detail and southern "personalism" are united in Dürer's *Arion on the Dolphin's Back.* A similar mingling of North and South is found in compositions of Josquin des Prés.

77

5. Sixteenth Century

Time of Internationalism

Consciousness of the spirit of rebirth invested the creative, social, and political worlds of Europe for two centuries. If the fifteenth was the time of trial and exploration, the sixteenth may best be described as the time of expansion and realization.

The major force shaping men's lives in the sixteenth century was the rise of truly secular thinking, as men began to challenge the Church's intellectual domination. On October 31, 1517, Martin Luther nailed to the church door of the court at Wittenberg his ninety-five theses calling for a reformation of church practices. Within two decades Henry VIII of England had broken with Rome over his divorce from Catherine of Aragon. In 1541 John Calvin delivered his protest at Geneva. Warfare, massacre, and persecution accompanied the birth of the new Protestant faith and its spread throughout Europe, as they had the birth of Christianity itself fifteen hundred years before.

A cultural trend was clear, however. Art and philosophy were becoming more and more independent from the church as center of learning and cultural determinant. (Even in the previous century, stirrings of the new spirit had been discernible as perspective came into painting and tonality into music.) Protestantism had a provocative influence on the new spirit. But Protestantism's concerns were those of the theologian, not of the artist. Painting in particular received little impetus from reformation doctrines. Like the ancient Hebrews, the leaders of the new church barred any representation of sacred personages. "God's majesty may not be corrupted by fantasies," was Calvin's doctrine. Thus, the Protestant painter and sculptor were forced to look elsewhere than the church for support and patronage, and for subject matter too.

In music, the effect of Protestantism was more positive and direct. Luther's original intent was a new kind of religious observance within the confines of the existing church, with certain elements retained from the Latin service side by side with new music of greater simplicity, appealing to and participated in by the congregation. This new music was the *chorale*, a simple and accessible melody harmonized entirely in block chords, without counterpoint, and rhythmically uncomplex. The Lutheran chorales, the bulwark of

80

the new church in Germany, were later to provide composers with a basis for some of their most important music.

In France, too, the new church music was conceived as something simpler, more immediate, more natural than the body of complex polyphony used in the Roman Church. Calvin called for banishment of the Latin service and a return to the ideals of the early Christians who sang the praises of God in the Psalms. Some of the most important composers of the time, notably Claude Le Jeune and Claude Goudimel, set to music the Psalms of the Huguenot Psalter which were in rhymed French translations. As with the Lutheran chorales, the melodies are simple and clear, and every word is intended to be heard. There is some contrapuntal movement in the inner parts.

The salient feature of the music of Protestantism was its immediacy. Aside from the texts, it would be difficult to tell it from the purely secular music of its time. In a sense, this emergence of a secular art meant a triumph for the Italian artistic ideal over the ideals of the North. It was in Italy that the love of pure beauty seemed to flourish at its most palpable, and this love warmed the hearts of the northerners who journeyed south to experience it first hand. We have seen this happen already in the case of Josquin des Prés and Albrecht Dürer. In the sixteenth century the cross-feeding of North and South produced a manner of expression in both music and the visual arts that was to create the world's first true artistic internationalism.

The spirit was international in that it involved creators of many nationalities. What held these men together was the heightened quest for naturalistic expression, which in its broadest sense knows no national boundaries. In the visual arts the rise of naturalism meant, primarily, the decline of Gothic symbolism, distortion, and "secret" devices; in music, naturalism meant the end of the equally secret constructive devices—so beloved by the Netherlanders at the end of the fifteenth century—in favor of the kind of music that seemed to embody the natural flow of human song.

The expansiveness of Renaissance art was manifested particularly in a new sense of space. The creator considered space a vital element both within his

81

work and surrounding it. We can observe the beginnings of the feeling for space as far back as the fourteenth-century Giotto, whose figures are the first to exist in open-air settings. The Van Eycks brought to their work a heightened sense of horizon, of background and foreground in relationship.

Probably the studies that most strikingly epitomize the quest for naturalness are to be found in the notebooks of Leonardo da Vinci. They are full of observations on rendering the human form, on light, shade, and perspective. They strike today's student of art as a statement of independence for the painter, as signaling the birth of "modern" techniques. But even before Leonardo the trend toward these techniques can be observed. It is seen early in the fifteenth century in the paintings of Fra Angelico, who began as an adherent of the archaic, flat, depersonalized style, but who showed in his later works a

82

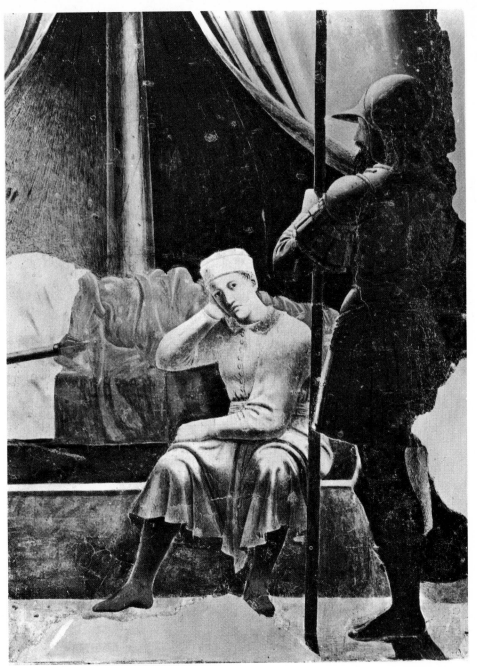

*O*pposite: Fra Angelico's *Birth of St. Nicholas of Bari* shows the persistence of flat perspective in its many geometric planes. Left: A section of Piero della Francesca's *Identification of the True Cross* illustrates the developing tendency to depict individualistic facial expressions.

83

strong concern for establishing planes at varying distances.

Immediately thereafter came Piero della Francesca, who brought light beams into his paintings, often from unexpected angles, to enhance the vivid coloration of his figures. In Piero's work we sense the workings of a scientific mind applying itself to the new problems; his groupings, and his figures themselves, are so precise in their shaping as to recall the techniques of the finest Greek sculptors, and yet they breathe with Renaissance naturalness. Paolo Uccello, another Italian whose early training had been along Gothic lines, heightened the effect of the newly discovered techniques by a fantastic and original use of slashing colors and complex perspectives in his late works.

Awareness of space was not confined to painting. Architects and civic planners, too, began late in the fifteenth century to think in terms of perspective, of leading the eye to a central point from long distances back. The Gothic cathedral was planned in terms of internal space, often on a grandiose scale, but the buildings themselves were often crowded onto plots of land hardly greater than their own exterior dimensions. Renaissance planners began to surround their great buildings with air and light so that the building itself became merely an element in a large design.

In music, too, the concept of space was united with, and inextricably joined to, the quest for simplicity and naturalness. To Venice came composers from the North, emulating the example of Josquin des Prés, and there, inspired by the grand design of the Basilica of San Marco and the huge piazza in front of it, they created music designed to fill its dimensions. To perform it, groups of singers and instrumentalists were stationed to answer and echo each other across a given area. The music itself, like all the music from the North, was polyphonic, but with so many voices in so great a space, the need to maintain clarity brought about a much simpler, more flowing kind of polyphony than we encounter in the complex works of Obrecht and Ockeghem. Thus, at the dawn of the sixteenth century, the synthesis achieved by Josquin—that between Flemish complexity and Italian euphony—became the prevailing musical manner.

*N*ote, in Fra Bartolomeo's *Angel of the Annunciation* (above, detail), the striking sense of movement, and (right), in Mantegna's *The Agony in the Garden,* the great depth of perspective together with a contrapuntal crowding of narrative elements.

84

As in painting, Italy became the center of the musical world in the new century. But it was, strangely, a center for immigrants. Not since Landino, late in the fourteenth century, had Italy produced an important native composer, nor would there be one until nearly the end of the Renaissance. Into the gap poured musicians from the North, with the result that musical leadership migrated practically overnight to the Italian peninsula.

The prime influence was, of course, the Roman Church—rich, illustrious, stable and serene on the surface, although deeply troubled by the Reformation movements in Germany, France, and England. Complementing Rome as musical centers were the large noble palaces throughout Italy, all with private chapels well equipped for music, as well as the culturally oriented cities of Florence and Venice. All these were potent lures for non-Italian composers.

In painting and in music, Venice became the center for experimentation. Adrian Willaert, the Netherlander who developed the broad, echoing Venetian choral style, was the first of a number of his countrymen who gave that city its true musical individuality. His successors in musical experimentation, including a "school" begun late in the century by native Italians Andrea Gabrieli and his nephew Giovanni, explored even more daring effects for answering masses of sound: choruses, groups of brass instruments, and combinations of voices and instruments. In the works of the Gabrielis we find not only echo effects, but even more subtle contrasts between groups playing loudly and answering groups playing softly. This was the first time in music that composers specified the desired dynamic level of a performance.

This increasing subtlety in the use of musical space parallels, so to speak, the growing mastery over perspective that can be traced in Italian painting. Starting in the fifteenth century with the works of Uccello and della Francesca, and continuing in the sixteenth century with the painters of the Venetian school, we can observe increasing assurance and audacity in the way painters controlled the space within a canvas. In the paintings of Titian, for example, we are made conscious not only of space but of movement within that space, of tilted perspective and unsymmetrical groupings. The work of Tintoretto,

*B*asilica of San Marco in Venice (opposite) is a veritable museum of styles ranging from Byzantine mosaic through medieval distorted sculpture, to details added in the Renaissance. Below: Cup ornamented in gold, enamel, and pearls, designed by Benvenuto Cellini for the Raspigliosi family.

87

*S*erenity, order, refinement, and balance of design are exemplified in the paintings of Raphael, whose work reflects the Italianate love of mellifluous harmony. Above: Detail from his *Parnassus;* right: *Madonna and Child Enthroned.*

the master of the late Renaissance in Venice, shows such control over light, shade, color, and object that we almost cease to be aware of the flat surface of the canvas, and become completely taken with a sense of expanse, of distance. Loud, soft, echo; light, shadow, horizon; in sixteenth-century Venice the arts of the painter and the composer seem almost interchangeable.

The dynamic flexibility of the Venetians represents only one side of Italian art in the High Renaissance, however. In that age of revived interest in the classic heritage of Greece and Rome there existed the same duality between the pathos and the ethos—the emotion and the restraint—that typified Greek thought at the time of Pericles. As an antithesis to the bursting, spatial concepts of the Gabrielis and Tintoretto there is the formal, symmetrical aspect of Italian art, coupled with a pursuit of gentle, refined sweetness. This is exemplified late in the fifteenth century in the paintings of Botticelli, so wonderfully delicate in their tracery, with a Venus that seems the absolute translation into paint of the highest ideals of the classic ethos. Botticelli's understanding of perspective was no less accomplished than that of Piero, but his paintings use it in a different way. His lines are clean, spatially organized yet static. And this quality we find *in excelsis* in the popular works of the best known of the Italian classicists, Raphael. His works are certainly more naturalistic than those of Botticelli; his figures are flesh-and-blood, not ethereal. And yet, in his passion for symmetry and order, Raphael also "freezes" his paintings, purposely denying them the free movement so strongly cultivated by the Venetians.

Ethos also governed the music of certain composers, above all, the last great exponent of Italian Renaissance polyphony, Giovanni da Palestrina. The serene and balanced logicality of this music represents the "classic" side of the Renaissance. His restrained harmonies are free of almost any trace of externalized passion. The sense of movement comes, instead, from a steadily controlled momentum created by the interweaving of graceful polyphonic lines— the techniques developed by the Netherlanders more than a century before, now made Italianate in the simplest and gentlest meaning of the term.

Although Italy was the artistic capital of Europe in the sixteenth century,

88

89

this cannot be taken to imply a failure of creativity in other countries. France, in particular, was able to keep its finest artists, to support them and provide them with a favorable artistic climate. Thus, there developed in France a small but important "school" embracing many arts, in contact with Italy and yet distinctly removed from Italian ideals.

If we can speak of Renaissance Italy as a land where scholarship thrived, particularly the study of the ancient past, and a land in which the artistic ideals embraced both naturalism and passion, we can also say of contemporary France that its artistic temperament imposed upon its own view of the classic past an element of individualistic fancy and charm. The intricately detailed mid-century paintings of the so-called Fontainebleau School are infused with this elegant fantasy.

Musically, too, sixteenth-century France gave itself to fanciful design. Aside from the brief, mellifluous pieces in the Huguenot Psalter, the major efforts of French Renaissance composers were in the direction of the *chanson,* an uncomplicated, but highly artistic popular song. Its basic texture was polyphonic, but here—as in Italy—the polyphony was greatly loosened, tempered to the elegant, not too intellectual taste of aristocratic audiences.

One of the genial features of the chanson was its occasional incorporation of sections with actual pictorial intent. Clément Jannequin created long, elaborate "program chansons" in which the voices might be called upon to imitate the birds heard outside a beloved's window, or, perhaps, the sounds of war: the ta-ran-ta-ra of horns, the throbbing of drums, the flight of arrows and musket balls. Nobody could call this sort of thing absolute naturalness; it is naturalism once removed, tempered with the highest wit and fantasy.

In France the art of the dance was so strongly rooted as to become almost a second national language. We have already seen how, in medieval times, dance elements became intertwined even in liturgical observances. Not until the sixteenth century, however, did the demands of the dance become strong enough to attract the attention of the serious composer. Now we begin to find dance music emerging as an important art form in itself.

90

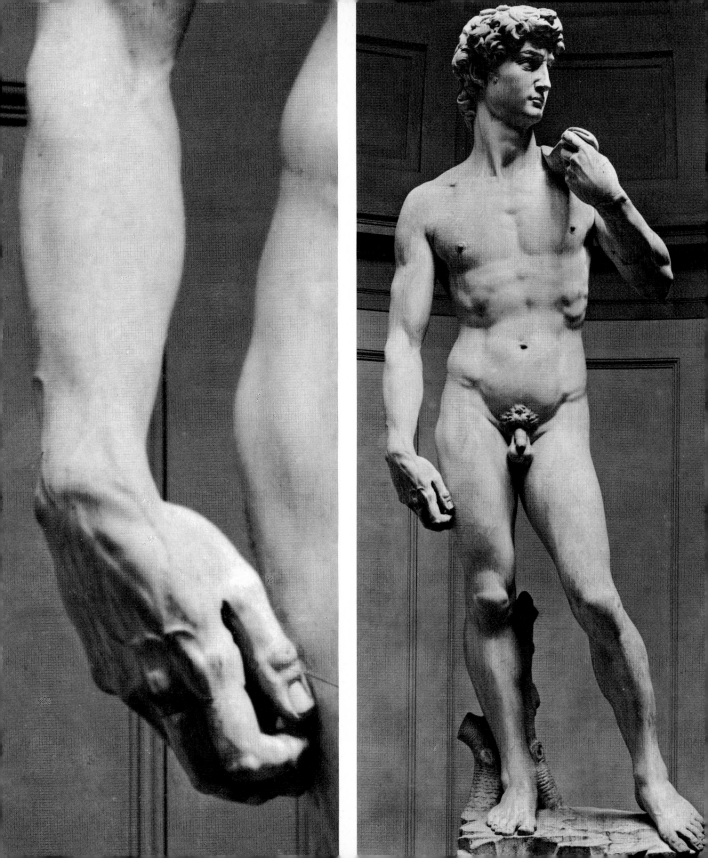

94

The typical courtly dance was actually a pair of dances, the first slow and the second fast; *pavan* and *gaillard* was a common pairing. Composers wrote movements for a solo instrument or, perhaps, a small ensemble of strings and winds. The music was simple in texture, graceful and tuneful in style. What is most important is that sometimes these pairs were musically related. The fast dance would be melodically and harmonically similar to the preceding slow dance, changed only in rhythm and pace. In this was the simple beginning of an important instrumental music technique, the *variations*.

THE LATE RENAISSANCE

In any artistic era that can be circumscribed and defined, it is fascinating to watch in historical perspective the slow and subtle turn from one artistic ideal to another. In the first half of the sixteenth century, as we have seen, Italian artistic expression was in equilibrium between the asymmetrical naturalism, expressed along lines that began in the preceding century with Angelico and Uccello and continued into the Venetian school, and the ideal of symmetry epitomized by Raphael, to some extent the heir of Botticelli. Late in the century, however, the balance seems to have been weighted heavily in favor of the former ideal, and the artist who did most to cause this shift was the supreme genius, Michelangelo.

He was, in all his work in all media, primarily a sculptor. Even in his paintings there is a surge of vitality, as if the figures were tensely striving to leave the canvas. As with his Venetian predecessors, Michelangelo created his figures as bodies occupying space. Now, these figures seem not merely to occupy the space, but to threaten and defy it, ready to explode into it. Sometimes it is the emotion of action. Just as often, as in the late, rough-cut Pietà sculptures in Florence and Milan, it is an inner, mystical, numbed emotion. Sometimes, as in the design for the architectural group on the Roman Campidoglio, the response is one of awe. This effect of tension is achieved through a masterful command of distortion. It is, if you will, a supernaturalism, a movement one step beyond the refined naturalness of his predecessors, whereby an element in

Michelangelo's David (pages 92 and 93) embodies the sense of arrested motion which the artist strove for in all his mature work. Note, in the two details, the eyes that force the viewer's gaze toward the antagonist, and the restrained fury of the hand. Opposite: Mystical lighting and angular arrangement of table give to Tintoretto's Last Supper a dynamism markedly different from mood of Leonardo's familiar version.

95

a painting or a sculptured group is distorted to move the attention forward, to create a sense of imbalance and, therefore, of motion. Sometimes the mere profusion of images crowded together into a seemingly small space is enough in itself to create this same sense of breathless, forward-moving urgency.

The art of Michelangelo epitomizes the general late-Renaissance tendency to heightened emotional expression in the arts. We find it even in some of the Venetian painters. By the use of oblique perspective and unsymmetrical arrangements, Titian and Tintoretto infused many of their paintings with sweep, urgency, even inner ecstasy.

The musical form which most directly embodied this sense of emotional immediacy and urgency was the *madrigal* as developed in Italy around 1550. The madrigal is a secular song, usually of highly personal nature (love requited or unrequited, love symbolized or actualized). Its prevailing style is polyphonic. Indeed, its first practitioners were among the same northerners who came to Venice and established there the polyphonic sacred style.

However, the poignancy of the madrigal texts—some of which were drawn from Italy's greatest poets, including Dante and Petrarch—demanded a far different mode of expression than did the Latin texts of the church. Composers indulged in fanciful and daring harmonic devices. Particular words of high passion might be underlined by a sudden introduction of a dissonant note, or a plunge by one or all voices from a high to a low register.

Naturally, these small-scale works are hardly fit comparisons for the vast emotional creations of Michelangelo. And yet they partake of the same spirit and they represent the same emotional intensification of earlier artistic techniques. In their use of musical devices of definite shock value—dissonance, change of register, perhaps a sudden irregular rhythm—they break away strongly from the serene, natural flow of both secular and sacred music prior to their time, toward an immediacy, a passion that was as unique in the realm of music as the emotional intensity of Michelangelo was in the visual arts.

The madrigal, combining as it did the refinements of musical and poetic passion with a strongly pictorial element, came to symbolize the highest cul-

96

97

*A*lmost a century separates Grünewald's Eisenheim Altarpiece (right) and El Greco's *Vision of St. John* (below), yet both artists achieved a feeling of great mystery and passion by the use of unusual spotlighting, emotionally distorted figures, and indeterminate perspectives. Both painters were largely untouched by the Italianate mainstream, and they are among the great individualists of the Renaissance.

tural attainment in the eyes of cultivated Italians. It became the elegant home entertainment; families and groups of friends sang madrigals after supper.

The madrigal stood as a closely contained drama, a single passionate scene. From it grew an even more elaborate entertainment, the *madrigal-comedy*, which told a longer story and was pantomimed by actors while connected madrigals were sung by an offstage chorus. Some of these entertainments were extremely complex and often quite witty, including episodes in dialect. Although there was no attempt in these works to differentiate between the characters, the relationship between this kind of musical-dramatic entertainment and the true opera of the ensuing century is obvious.

The madrigal, developed in Italy, later took root in England as well, first brought by composers who migrated from the South, then composed by Englishmen themselves. Like Italy, England had a noble heritage of great lyric poetry, including Shakespeare's and that of lesser lyricists like Sir Philip Sidney. Many of the first English madrigals were almost exact paraphrases of Italian models, but in the hands of the great madrigalists Thomas Morley, John Wilbye, and others, the form developed an individuality and a repertory of passionate musical devices all its own.

Is not this musical and pictorial distortion in the quest of emotionalism something of a throwback to Gothic ideals? The question might well be asked and, indeed, historians have often applied to this style a term also encountered in descriptions of the late Gothic: mannerism. In the late sixteenth century, as in the late fourteenth, the artist exhibits a heightened involvement with personal fantasy and secret symbolic visions.

In the paintings of the Italian Caravaggio and of Spain's El Greco, at the very end of the Renaissance, can be found even more of this mystic quality. In both, for example, there is a purposeful use of unreal, lurid lighting, and of faces and bodies that twist and writhe with inner passion. The elongation of figures in El Greco's paintings bears even closer resemblance to Gothic ideals. Even in certain works of the High Renaissance, Tintoretto's *Last Supper*, for example, there is a mannerism in the approach to lighting and perspective.

100

Distortion of line and form was used also by the German painter, Mathias Grünewald, as in the *Crucifixion* from his Eisenheim altarpiece, which produces in the viewer feelings of profound disturbance.

Distortion affected music, too, late in the century, as many composers took a new, free approach to the use of dissonance. The great Fleming Orlando di Lasso, who lived for a while in almost every major musical center of Europe and wrote prolifically in almost all prevalent musical styles, brought some of this passion into many of his scores, even those composed for church use. There can also be found a high degree of wild, passionate expression—achieved through devices usually found in the madrigal—in the church compositions of Tomás Luis de Victoria, a Spaniard who spent much of his career as a composer at the Vatican. Like the madrigalists, Victoria used a striking dissonance treatment to underscore words of particularly somber or dramatic intent, and created thereby the same sort of introverted religious vision that can be found in the El Greco paintings.

Dissonance also appears in the work of one of the most fascinating musical personalities of the time, Don Carlo Gesualdo, prince of Venosa, (among whose accomplishments was the murder of his wife, for presumed infidelity). Gesualdo's madrigals, songs almost always dealing with excruciatingly tragic passions (and usually with texts by himself), have a sharply dissonant quality that still amazes musicians, considering that they are the work of a sixteenth-century composer. It is possible to find in his music harmonic progressions more characteristically associated with works of Richard Wagner, composed almost three centuries later.

The English also assumed this aspect of the Italian style in their wholesale adoption of the madrigal. Gesualdo's English counterpart was John Dowland, whose grieving madrigals also show a tendency toward passionate dissonance and long, heartrending melodies. In these songs there is so much emphasis on the top voice in the ensemble that they become almost solo pieces with accompaniment. Thus, Dowland early recognizes the poignance of the solo voice that was, not many decades later, to sweep through Europe and overshadow the entire concept of vocal polyphony for a long time to come.

William Byrd, who wrote both madrigals and sacred works, also employed to a large extent this free, passionate harmonic style. A composer whose reputation as a striking individualist seems to be growing rapidly today, Byrd took special delight in strong harmonic clashes between the voices of a polyphonic composition. One voice, for example, might sing an F sharp, followed soon after by another voice singing a "contradictory" F natural. Byrd's overall contrapuntal style was clearly in the Flemish-Italian manner, and yet this striking attitude toward harmony gives his music a strong, somewhat rough-cut flavor unmistakably his own.

INSTRUMENTAL MUSIC IN THE LATE RENAISSANCE

The beginnings of a true musical style intended for instruments rather than voices can be ascribed to the creators of the dance early in the sixteenth century, working in France and later by migration in Italy and Spain. Later in the century, however, there emerges for the first time an instrumental style that is not necessarily dance-determined, and in which the technical demands of the instruments themselves exert a definite shaping influence on the music.

By late in the century a luxuriant array of instruments was available in

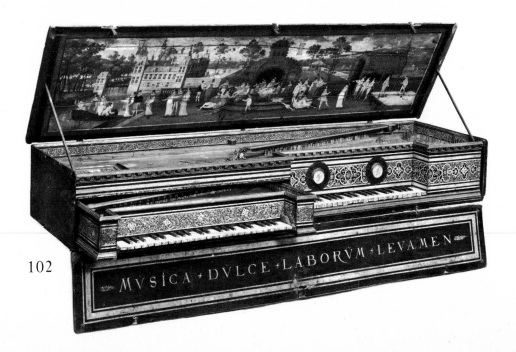

homes, churches, and public halls throughout Europe. There were the keyboard instruments, including the small virginals, spinet, clavichord, larger harpsichord, and organ. Among the stringed instruments there were the members of the viol family, ancestors of our present violin family, again available in varying sizes and often grouped together to form an ensemble known as a *consort*. Brass instruments—including the straight trumpet, the hunting horn, and the trombone—together with various kinds of flutes or recorders, oboes, and lower-pitched wind instruments, formed the body of village bands, along with percussion of all sizes, shapes, and degrees of portability. Finally, there was a large family of plucked stringed instruments, notably the lute.

It was thus apparent to composers that there were other performing forces under the sun besides the human voice. Vocal music, however, exerted a strong influence on the early attempts at instrumental style. The first true instrumental forms were clear models of polyphonic vocal pieces: madrigals, chansons, and more serious religious works. Gradually, however, two things began to happen. First, even the vocal-influenced works became freer in style, with the instrumentalists allowed to execute an increasing number of flourishes, runs, and other virtuosic passages. Second, new forms emerged that were no longer beholden to vocal models.

One of these was the *toccata*, usually conceived for a keyboard instrument, which was generally a brilliant piece, improvisatory in character, often quite extended, and clearly designed to exploit virtuosic skill. The other was the set of *variations*, in which a given melody, stated at the outset, was then restated with new accompanying figurations, thus becoming more and more complex. By the end of the sixteenth century, this technique, first heard in the paired French dance, had become one of the most elaborate musical exercises in the repertory, especially in the hands of English composers.

The history of artistic style marks the late Renaissance as the time when individual musical virtuosity developed. This may be expected in view of the general tenor of the entire era, which saw the emergence of the individual creator and thinker as a power in the universe.

*M*usic and painting come together in the ornate designs conceived by Renaissance craftsmen to adorn musical instruments of the time. This is a Flemish virginal of 1581, with double keyboard, a forerunner of the harpsichord.

103

6. The

Italian Baroque

*A*t this point—the close of the sixteenth century—we can discern two generally separate schools of musical expression in Europe: the Northern ideal, characterized by complexity, contrivance, and a certain aloofness; and the Southern, in which simplicity, emotional warmth, and immediacy are the major traits. The two ideals did not exist in isolation, however. Almost always, the work of an individual composer, or group of composers, represents a blending of the two.

This is to some extent an oversimplification and there are many exceptions. But it is a useful and generally accurate approach to musical history. It will be found no less applicable in the baroque era than in the Middle Ages and the Renaissance. Stated another way, the Southern, or specifically the Italian, musical ideal tends to regard the human voice, singing a clearly vocal melody, as the absolute, while the Northern ideal regards the voice, interchangeable with instruments, as the means toward expressing a more or less abstract design.

Art historians today tend to regard the baroque era not as a separate epoch, but as a further extension and intensification of trends apparent in the late Renaissance. The term "baroque" comes from the Portuguese word for an irregularly shaped pearl, and the key word there is "irregular." The baroque quality implies many things, but most of all it signifies a new breaking away from the classic ideal of symmetry and clear forms.

Thus, the mannerism in Italian art, first evident in the sculptures of Michelangelo, is an early expression of the baroque. So, too, are the distortion in El Greco's paintings and the dynamic, off-center perspective of Tintoretto. In these works one is confronted with a sense of space and the rushing of painted and sculptured figures to fill that space.

Baroque beginnings are found also in the architecture of the late Renaissance. The classic pillared façade merges, as in Vignola's Church of the Gesù begun in Rome in 1568, with a more dynamic shape, with great sweeping curves of masonry that seem to suggest an intense rhythm frozen only momentarily into stone, ready at any time to resume its surge.

106

Italian artists in the early seventeenth century were concerned with particularizing their subjects. For all his fury and tension, Michelangelo's David is still the idealized heroic figure. But the David of Bernini, carved a hundred and twenty years later, is the Biblical youth: a peasant with a peasant's face, whose fury is so palpable and all-embracing that one almost sees the invisible Goliath standing not far off. Caravaggio's St. Matthew sits in a tavern with foppish companions, and his answer to Jesus' summoning is so real and startled that one almost hears the "Who, me?" This heightened resemblance to the man on the street made the naturalism of the baroque even more palpable than the naturalism that was the ideal of the High Renaissance.

It was this desire for naturalness of expression and closeness to human emotions that led a group of Florentine intellectuals around 1590 to institute a search for a new kind of music. These men, who called their group the *camerata*, were amateurs from all walks of life, including a few musicians, poets, and painters, drawn together in a study of Greek drama and philosophy, as were many aristocrats of the time. But the principal concern of the camerata was drama, and specifically the finding of a way to express the spirit of ancient lyric tragedy through the inflections of the human voice. The music of the time, they felt, was ill-suited to dramatic purposes. The complex counterpoint of the madrigal obscured the sense of the words and forced music into artificial rhythmic patterns which violated the laws of poetic declamation. Vincentio Galilei, father of the astronomer, sounded the doctrine in his *Dialogue on Old and New Music*. In it, Galilei called for the creation of a new style of singing, the *recitative*, in which a single voice could express the passions of the poem to a free and flexible rhythm determined by the words themselves, accompanied in the most discreet manner by a keyboard instrument or lute, which merely supplied the supporting harmony.

The baroque manner in music, therefore, began as an evocation of classicism. The transition, unlike that in the visual arts from Renaissance to baroque, was violent and revolutionary. Even so, the learned iconoclasts of Florence could have little idea of the scope and implications of their reform.

107

*I*n two early baroque works, Caravaggio's *The Summoning of Matthew* and Bernini's David, one is struck first of all by the models themselves: no longer the idealized Renaissance figures, but people who seem to be drawn from the streets of the artists' own times.

The first experiments by the camerata were short, simple songs. The vocal line was written out, while the keyboard accompaniment was merely sketched: a single note in the bass with figures below it to indicate the harmony, and from which the player could improvise a certain amount of ornamentation. This bass line for keyboard was called *figured bass*, *thorough bass*, or *basso continuo*, terms which historians sometimes apply to the baroque period as a whole. The conception of music as polarized between a melodic line and a harmonic accompaniment, represents one of the crucial revolutions in the panorama of music.

The composers of the period hastened to apply the new concept to drama of greater length and substance, and in 1600 two members of the camerata, the poet-musicians Giulio Caccini and Jacopo Peri, set to music a pastoral-mythological text of their own creation, *Euridice*. The choice of subject matter is significant. For one thing, a neo-Greek revival demanded a Greek subject, and for another the legend of Orpheus and Eurydice is the story par excellence of the triumph of music over the forces of blackness.

By today's standards, the early examples of *dramma per musica*, or *opera* (the terms were used interchangeably), are not very interesting. The creators were enthusiastic amateurs, and their obsession with the stark simplicity of the

110

new style created a musical line with little melodic interest. Chances are that without composers of greater skill these experiments in *stile rappresentativo* ("representative" or "theatrical" style) would have had little future. Fortunately for the art of music, however, the supreme Italian composer of his day was attracted to the new style, and the history of opera as an important art form began in 1607 with the production of *L'Orfeo*, by Claudio Monteverdi, at the court at Mantua.

Monteverdi was already famous as one of the finest creators of madrigals in the late Renaissance manner. He seemed to grasp the new style intuitively, but he also had the superb dramatic instinct to recognize the limitations of a whole evening of thinly accompanied recitative. The greatness of *L'Orfeo* lies partly in its canny synthesis of old and new practices. There are madrigalesque choruses interspersed in the action which provide both dramatic and musical contrast. There are moments of passion in which the constantly flexible recitative is subtly altered to a more shapely and regular melody of great poignance. The lament of Orpheus in the second act, for example, when he first hears of the death of Eurydice, and the long appeal to Charon to ferry him into Hades, are true songs of great lyric beauty.

Here are the beginnings of opera as it is known today. In *L'Orfeo* there is

111

a duality in the way the story is told: the free, speech-derived recitative sung by the characters as they act out the story itself, and the lyrical *aria* in which the action stops and the characters sing of their state of mind, and in which purely musical considerations dominate.

Moreover, Monteverdi surrounded this vocal action with a wide range of orchestral color. He fleshed out the basic accompaniment of harpsichord and a few strings with groups of brass and wind instruments, many more strings, and an organ. He also used tone color to underline a mood. For instance, much of the action in the infernal regions is accompanied by somber sonorities in the brass, heightening the mystery of these scenes.

Finally, Monteverdi brought to this opera the element of virtuosity. In order to underscore the dramatic action, the singers are called upon to tax their resources, to indulge in trills and wide-ranging ornamentations. The surrounding instruments are no less active. Just as the tense, contorted lines of baroque sculpture and architecture suggest an imminent explosion into action, so also do the convoluted vocal lines of Monteverdi give the impression of violent feelings lurking just below the surface. Such is the power of music to enhance and intensify the written word.

The concept of opera brought to music a new kind of dramatic power and a new spaciousness. Everything about the form was on a grander scale than any previous kind of music. For one thing, it lasted longer. A single opera was a full evening's entertainment, whereas the most expansive musical form of the Renaissance, the Mass, lasted less than an hour.

Furthermore, there were other kinds of grandeur in the new art. It engaged the crafts of the scenic designer and the costumer, and they usually were encouraged to think extravagantly. The emotions depicted were extreme, and the singers could summon the full range of gesticulation to drive home the points they sought to make vocally. Opera required production in large halls where the stage and the orchestra area could accommodate the composer's demands.

Opera spread throughout Italy. In 1637 the first public opera house was opened in Venice, where Monteverdi was then living. There was also, in Rome,

Guido Reni, another baroque artist whose work might be called the "calendar art" of its day, did, after all, flourish at a time when music, too, was making its appeal (through operatic virtuosity primarily) to mass tastes. This is Reni's *Bacchus*.

113

*T*wo baroque artists
come to grips with classic legends.
Left: Poussin's *Orpheus
and Eurydice* in an Arcadian setting;
above: a stage set by
Jacques Callot for a play (or perhaps
an opera) in which the forces
of Hades arm for battle on behalf
of the sorceress Circe.

115

a school of operatic composers who were particularly eager to present musico-dramatic entertainments on a lavish scale requiring complex stage mechanisms and frequent changes of scene.

Grandeur and spaciousness were very much a part of Roman life early in the seventeenth century. Bernini's plan for the piazza in front of Saint Peter's used space in a new and dazzling way. The lines suggest movement, far more so than those, say, of the Piazza San Marco in Venice; all was designed for sweep. His two curving colonnades swept the eye forward to the building itself and up to Michelangelo's mighty dome; the greatest church of the Catholic world was no longer merely a grand building, but the focus of a far grander scheme. This dynamism in the use of space had, of course, been suggested in the previous century. Early in the baroque era, it became intensified.

Instrumental music was not excluded from the baroque sense of spaciousness and dynamic movement. These elements are found in the purely instrumental works of Girolamo Frescobaldi, a Roman organist and one of the great Italian composers of his time. Organist at Saint Peter's from 1608 until his death in 1643, Frescobaldi caught much of the expansiveness and emotional intensity of the period in his solemn, mystical-sounding organ pieces.

In some ways, his style recalls certain of the musical practices in use at the end of the Renaissance. His music is contrapuntal, beholden in some of its external features to the techniques of Palestrina. But this is a new kind of contrapuntal writing. For one thing, it is completely idiomatic to the organ, with a range of virtuosity that would be unthinkable in vocal music. For another, the use of dissonance and shifting harmonies bespeaks a new freedom.

The new dramatic musical idiom also came to permeate sacred music. The *oratorio* was developed in Rome as the churchly counterpart to opera. Its name comes from the fact that it was performed in the oratory of the church, and it was in reality an unstaged opera on a Biblical or moral subject, with the place of dramatic action and scenery taken by a narrator who set the stage for the "actors" with occasional passages of recitative. The chorus was also prominent in oratorio, more so than in opera, singing from time to time what might be

116

called a moral commentary on the action, or else participating more actively as a background for the drama embodied by the soloist. The choral effects were often quite grand, with several groups of singers used for antiphonal effects, as in the older polychoral works from Venice.

As opera became an increasingly popular form of entertainment among elegant and cultured Italian audiences, it underwent a number of stylistic changes. In general, the trend was toward thinner music, uncomplex harmonically and crowd-pleasing. The principal interest became focused on the lyrical passages—the arias—which became longer, more formalized in structure, and often burdened with a huge amount of coloratura to please the singers cast in

117

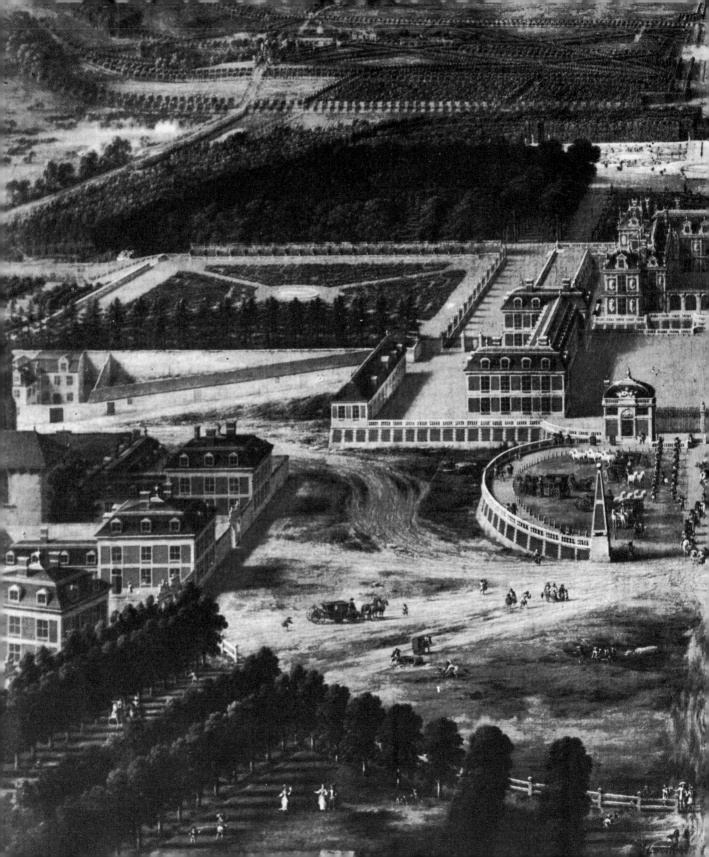

Monteverdi's late works begin to show this trend, although on a high artistic level. His masterpiece, *The Coronation of Poppaea*, written for Venice in 1642, is far more overtly lyrical and graceful than the passionate *Orfeo* of thirty-five years before. But in the hands of this dramatic genius the so-called *bel canto* style (that is, "beautiful singing," characterized by a flowing and shapely vocal line) still rang with dramatic overtones.

In general, however, the bel canto repertory was musically rather thin. Its standard of taste was somewhat less discriminating than that set by Monteverdi. In its sentimental prettiness it might be called the musical companion to the paintings of one of the most popular Italian painters of the mid-seventeenth century, Guido Reni. These works, rigid and formalized to the point where significance is overwhelmed, represent a certain sad corruption at a time when the desire to please large masses of the populace temporarily halted the search for heightened expression.

But if Italy suffered a brief stagnation in the mid-baroque, the ideals fomented there early in the era were spreading to fertile ground in other countries throughout Europe. One of Monteverdi's closest admirers was the German Heinrich Schütz, the first major exponent of the baroque manner in his native country. All of Schütz's extant compositions are religious works. He was the first Lutheran composer to enhance the unadorned repertory of his church with music of genuine expanse and originality. His major works are, in reality, short sacred operatic arias and scenes.

Other Italian baroque influences also appear in Schütz's works. He was strongly influenced by the Roman manner, especially the colossal effect obtained through the use of great masses of choral and instrumental sound.

France favored the lighter, less complex side of the Italian manner. Several troupes of Italian operatic performers visited Paris, and one of their number remained there to found almost singlehandedly a French operatic style. Born Giovanni Battista Lulli, he changed his name to Jean Baptiste Lully, and dominated French musical life for nearly four decades until his death in 1687.

120

The French found little to admire in the dynamic aspects of baroque art. Their painters remained rooted in Renaissance classicism. Raphael, far more than Michelangelo, was their master, and their own exponent of Raphael's statuesque classicism was Nicolas Poussin. Other painters, too, notably Claude Lorrain, preserved in their elegant canvases the cool, reserved style of an earlier era in defiance of the passion of men like Bernini. French dramatists as well—Racine and Corneille most importantly—based their plays on classic subject matter and treated it in the classic manner.

Lully's French operas partake of this spirit. Like the reserved, clean lines of Lorrain's *Pastoral*, their musical style is simple, open, and clear. The rhythms are often close to those of the dance, since this was and always has been a major element of French taste. Lully's subjects, too, are mythological, and they are treated with great musical reserve. His music is typical of the whole course of French art in the seventeenth century. As dictated to a large extent by the tastes of the monarch, Louis XIV, it sidestepped almost entirely the powerful stresses of the Italianate passion.

Louis' tastes prescribed an abjuration of the ideals of the early Italian baroque in favor of a more classic concept which, interestingly enough, Italy itself was soon to follow. Under his patronage were built two of the world's

121

*O*ften, magnificence of mid-baroque opera lay not so much in its music as in the scenic effects its creators wisely included. Splendor marked performance of Cesti's *Il Pomo d'Oro* at Court theater in Vienna (above) and Lully's *Theseé* at Versailles.

great architectural treasures, the royal palace at Versailles and, in its finished form, the Palace of the Louvre in Paris. Both represent the triumph of classicism over the dynamic Italian asymmetry. The dominant spirit of each edifice is classic, but the size, grace, and grandeur of their total design was without modern precedent.

Louis' musical preferences were of like nature. For the royal chapels, Lully and his colleagues Michel de Lalande and Marc Antoine Charpentier composed music that was massive in its total sonority, static and uncomplex in its detail. The object clearly was to fill a structure with masses of rich sound, with detail-work consisting largely of formalized ornamentation applied to the vocal line. Blocky and unimaginative though much of this repertory seems, it succeeds brilliantly in its purpose.

One other country came strongly under the spell of the Italian style and met it, musically at least, on its own terms. The dominant English composer of the baroque, Henry Purcell, brought home from his Italian visits a deep and abiding respect for the new dramatic style, and produced a brilliant repertory of his own in this manner. Purcell was, like his forebear William Byrd, a product of the English tradition of harmonic daring and strong dissonance used for dramatic purposes. Many of his sacred compositions, such as the anthems and odes composed while he was choirmaster at the Chapel Royal, are laid out in the grandiose manner of the Roman baroque pieces, with arias, recitatives, and choruses. They have, however, a kind of introspective, chromatic style, traceable partly to Purcell's exposure to the music of Monteverdi and partly to the traditions of English music.

Purcell's true worth as a dramatic composer is revealed in his secular dramatic music: the short opera *Dido and Aeneas* and the various sets of incidental music composed for the London theater. Here the fusion of English and Italian styles produces some of the most powerful and poignant dramatic music of the age. *Dido*, although composed for amateur performers and set to a text of rather appalling mediocrity, is in its deeply dramatic quality the first work composed since Monteverdi's *L'Orfeo* that is worthy to stand beside it.

123

THE LATE ITALIAN BAROQUE

Bernini and Monteverdi were, in a sense, the beginning and also the culmination of the pure baroque in Italy. The ideal of passion and unspoken emotional intensity that began with Michelangelo lost its thrust after these men. This is why scholars have difficulty defining the limits of the baroque era. The ideals of the second half are decidedly different from those of its beginning.

Again, the antitheses seem to be the pathos and the ethos, the Dionysian and Apollonian, in a kind of uneasy balance. The Italian baroque manner began in an outburst of pure emotion, controlled on the surface but present by implication. As the era progressed emotion was made more and more explicit; dynamism was less in evidence, sentimentality more so.

These new artistic developments, especially as they accompanied the spread of opera from Italy to France and England, had decidedly social causes. For the first time in the history of the Western arts, the matter of popularity and the effect of public taste upon the creator become decisive considerations.

The medieval artist—composer, painter, or sculptor—usually drew his support from church authorities, and worked toward enhancing in his own way the religious message. In the Renaissance a certain amount of artistic patronage passed into the hands of the secular individual: the aristocrat who maintained his own chapel and music room, and a great palace with walls that demanded decoration. For him and his guests were created the great secular paintings of the Renaissance, the dances, chansons, madrigals, and instrumental pieces. Operas, too, began under aristocratic patronage. Monteverdi's *L'Orfeo* was written for a wedding ceremony at the court of Mantua.

*F*ocal point of Bernini's design for St. Peter's Square in Rome is lavish Altar of the Chair of St. Peter in the basilica, with its stone "canopy" crowned with trumpeting angel hosts.

All this changed with the opening of the public opera houses and the intrusion of operatic elements into church services through the oratorio. The arts by the middle of the seventeenth century were extending their influence to the bourgeoisie whose tastes, if not axiomatically lower, are at least more diverse. Standards became, if not reduced, at least changed. Sentiment became infused with sentimentality. When the public could not be reached by the art of the creator, that was replaced (or at least disguised) by the art of the performer.

124

Virtuosity in any of the arts is not in itself a pejorative element, but as it became an end in itself, which happened for the first time in the seventeenth century, it required for its assimilation the development of new artistic ideals.

By midcentury the center of opera had moved from Venice and Rome to Naples. Neapolitan opera, whose most illustrious creator was Alessandro Scarlatti, sacrificed dramatic tension in favor of sensuous melody. Its composers pandered to the vocal virtuosos who were in turn lead on by public adoration. The recitative, which carried forward the action in a subtle, speech-like manner, was drastically foreshortened and sometimes even left to the helter-skelter improvisation of the singers. The emphasis was on the arias, formal and dramatically static. Here, everything focused on the voice. The orchestra was pared down to a small group of accompanying strings and a keyboard instrument playing the basso continuo, and there often were moments in which the singer was required to execute a brilliant unaccompanied *cadenza*, which further slowed the musico-dramatic momentum. It was a decorative art, en-

126

hanced by brilliant stage décor and elaborate costumes, but something of a comedown from the dynamic beginnings of opera.

Yet, Scarlatti was an excellent composer and he operated with great skill within the limitations of his medium. His melodic sense was keen and inventive, and he even allowed himself an occasional departure from the prevailingly bland harmonic style beloved by the Neapolitan opera-goers.

In the north of Italy there grew up an instrumental counterpart to the operatic school, one which became extremely important in the development of orchestral composition and performance throughout Europe. In Cremona, around 1670, Antonio Stradivari and his colleagues perfected the violin as an instrument capable of a far sweeter singing tone than the viols which were then the bulwark of the orchestra, and a group of composers began to explore the possibilities inherent in this new instrument, along with its lower-pitched relatives the viola and violoncello. Chief among them was Arcangelo Corelli, whose entire output consists of six collections of music for stringed instruments, solo or in groups, with basso continuo.

Instrumental music around 1650 was of several types, some of which could be traced back to vocal forms of the Renaissance, some not. In the former group were the *ricercàre*, based on the contrapuntal sacred works of the late sixteenth century, serious in tone and involving continuous imitation among the "voices"; and the *canzona*, also contrapuntal but lighter in style, somewhat akin to the madrigal, and made up of several short sections, each of which worked out its own short theme. In the latter group were the *fantasia*, or *capriccio*, also contrapuntal and based on the imitative working-out of a single melodic idea, but much more idiomatic to instruments than to voice; virtuoso pieces in an improvisatory style called *toccata;* works in a more-or-less stylized dance manner, either single or strung together as a *suite* or *partita;* there were also several kinds of variation groups in which a given melody repeats constantly with new and increasingly elaborate figuration, as for example in the *chaconne* or *passacaglia*, whose repeating melody is short and occurs in the bass line as a constant, with new ideas added above it. These forms occasionally overlapped, as in some

*I*n his *Allegory,* the little-known Italian baroque painter, Giovanni Benedetto Castiglione, created a canvas that epitomized the love of his contemporaries for mystery, symbolism, and nameless passion.

examples of partita where all the dances are variations of the same theme.

Out of these kinds of instrumental music grew the later forms which were exploited and developed by the northern Italian violin school. The canzona in particular suggested a multisectional composition in which the sections alternated in tempo, but in which each section (or movement) would be complete in itself.

Moreover, Corelli developed a kind of writing for strings which involved contrasts in the volume of sounds, a large group of instruments alternating with a smaller group. His thinking here was obviously inspired by the Venetian polychoral music of the late Renaissance or the Roman oratorios of the early baroque, both of which depended on contrasts among large and small groups of performers. In Corelli's hands this became the *concerto grosso*.

In addition to using the stringed instruments in groups, Corelli—a virtuoso violinist himself—composed works for solo violin accompanied by the keyboard continuo. In these the violinist became the clear counterpart of the Neapolitan opera singer, working out his part with considerable virtuosity, and following in slow movements a long, sensuous melodic line directly in the bel canto tradition. These were the *sonatas*, and when two soloists were involved above the accompanying keyboard part, it became the *trio sonata*.

Within each of his compositions, Corelli worked out a clear formal pattern. The movements themselves alternate, usually in a slow-fast-slow-fast pattern, and within each movement there is a clear ordering of events: a statement of a principal theme in the tonality of the movement, a change to a new tonality, and a gradual return. Some of his movements are, rhythmically, closely related to dance forms and patterns of the time. Others are abstract.

The basic symmetry of this kind of musical ordering is clearly related to the classic ideal: certainly it veers away from the dynamic and flexible ordering of the early baroque. Nor is Corelli the only creator with whom this is so. Many other artists in late-seventeenth-century Italy show in their work a reëmergence of the classic spirit. Its visual exponents were the architect Guarino Guarini and the painter Giovanni Tiepolo. Significantly, Guarini

128

was also a mathematician. His masterful Chapel of the Holy Shroud at Turin is a scientifically proportioned arrangement of complex materials, in its orderliness and symmetry quite alien to the baroque ideal. Tiepolo, too, in his serene decorative designs, such as the ceiling fresco for the Kaisersaal at Würzburg, combines a symmetry reminiscent of Raphael with a shower of elegant figuration. The effect is almost like a Corelli violin sonata made visual. There is in some of Tiepolo's work a persistence of Reni's sentimentality and obsession with virtuosity. But he, like Corelli, returned dignity to his art through the simplicity and nobility of his design, mingled with airy fantasy.

The new musical style was, above all else, serene, elegant, and fanciful.

130

In the generation following Corelli men like Antonio Vivaldi and a host of others, including Albinoni, Manfredini, Locatelli, Marcello, and Geminiani, carried Corelli's ideas onto new levels. The solo instruments—usually the violin, but sometimes a wind or brass—were given even more intricate figuration and thus turned into an idealized operatic voice of greater passion than ever before. Out of the Corelli concerto grosso grew the solo concerto, in which the contrast was between a single instrument and the full group of strings. In his most imaginative works Vivaldi accomplished remarkable things with the virtuosic style, as in his set of four concertos called *The Four Seasons*, in which solo violins are called upon to imitate the sounds of nature.

And one Italian of the time brought the element of instrumental virtuosity to the keyboard; Domenico Scarlatti, son of the operatic composer Alessandro. Composer to the Spanish court for most of his lifetime, Scarlatti produced some vocal music similar in style to that of his father. But his principal contribution was a series of over five hundred *studies* or sonatas for harpsichord solo, each of them consisting of a single movement, but usually composed in pairs or sets of three. What Corelli and Vivaldi accomplished for the violin in establishing standards of virtuosity and exploring a vast range of expressive possibilities, Scarlatti accomplished for the harpsichord early in the eighteenth century, in the waning years of that instrument's popularity.

Scarlatti's sonatas are, in fact, a catalogue of expressive devices. Many reflect his Spanish environment, using the instrument to imitate the sounds of guitars and even of processional bands. Others are more abstract, almost mystical. Some have sudden changes of harmony and are marked by a wildness of passion that is also partly Spanish, and partly a return to earlier baroque modes of expression. One thing is common to all, however, and it reflects the artistic mood of Scarlatti's own time. The sonatas are built on a clear and regular formal pattern, as are the concerti of Corelli and Vivaldi. Classicism, with its emphasis on clear organization and symmetry, is the dominant spirit in the late years of the Italian baroque.

The late Italian baroque manner, like that of the early years of the era,

Guarino Guarini's Chapel of the Holy Shroud at Turin, a barreled structure of such incredible complexity that the eye seems tricked into gazing on the infinite, is a compelling example of the way in which the late-baroque artist—architect as well as composer—made detail subjective.

131

found acceptance in other countries as well. Henry Purcell, in addition to his operatic works influenced by the earlier baroque, also brought back to England the instrumental styles of Italy, and composed large amounts of music for strings and solo harpsichord in the late manner. The German Georg Philipp Telemann composed prolifically in the Vivaldi style.

The supreme genius of the Italian manner was another German, who visited Italy early in his career and then settled in England: George Frederick Handel. Working in practically every mode of composition that had its genesis in the Italian baroque, Handel mastered them all to a degree not attained even by those who had invented the styles.

Handel composed the finest examples of Neapolitan opera. (The English audience was already greatly taken by this style, thanks to long visits by Neapolitan companies.) In these works, despite the occasional artificialities of the texts, his own powerful sense of the dramatic potential of harmony results in a depth of expression beyond the best in Alessandro Scarlatti and his disciples. Handel's English patrons accorded him unlimited facilities for staging his works on a lavish scale and he repaid them handsomely.

He also brought the baroque oratorio to its highest development. Most of his oratorios retain the old Roman device of a narrator to set the scene, but the narration itself becomes integrated into the dramatic scheme and the singer is given, in addition to recitative, arias of exceptional beauty. His choruses are massive at times, even more so than the Roman models, but he also had a brilliant feeling for the imaginative use of light-textured vocal ensembles for special effects. Certainly a chorus like "Let no rash intruder" in the oratorio *Solomon* bespeaks a style of vocal writing far more resourceful than that of the Italian mid-baroque.

Most importantly, Handel greatly increases the role played by the orchestra in his dramatic vocal compositions. As did Vivaldi in his *Four Seasons*, Handel often uses his orchestra in a kind of programmatic way. The depiction of the plagues visited upon the Egyptians in *Israel in Egypt* is a fine example of this fanciful manner, and the "Pastoral Symphony" in *Messiah* creates a par-

134

ticular atmosphere in the way it employs wind instruments.

His instrumental music is also strongly influenced by Italian models. The famous set of twelve concerti grossi, based on the Corelli works, are especially imaginative in the way elements of dance music alternate with more abstract designs. The famous *Water Music* is a series of dance movements scored for an ensemble of winds, brass, and strings, in which each movement follows the formal outline of a Corelli movement or a Scarlatti sonata, and in which the sonority of the scoring greatly enhances the effect.

The grandeur of Handel's musical designs and the range of his musical imagination made him immensely popular with the London public, and his fame continued long after his death. Indeed, his manner of composition was to cast its influence on the course of English music for almost a century, besides inspiring such later continental composers as Haydn and Mendelssohn.

Handel's was an age of grandeur. England had by his time assimilated enough of the Italian manner to have effected some degree of accommodation with it. At the same time that Handel's Italianate style reached its zenith, there was also taking place a great architectural revival based on Italian classicism. Its leader was the architect Sir Christopher Wren, who seemed able in his finest structures to approach a synthesis of the finest Italianate gestures of many centuries. His rebuilding of Saint Paul's Cathedral, for example, is a smooth reconciliation of ancient Roman designs with the baroque dynamism of Michelangelo and Bernini. Thus, Wren managed to sidestep, as surely as did Handel himself, the more excessive aspects of the Italian baroque and to concentrate on the strengths of the Southern heritage.

Other Italianate elements were brought to England by the Venetian painter Canaletto, who settled there for a time. With a series of "postcards" depicting the sights of Venice, he kept the enthusiastic English constantly aware of the beauties of the South. Like the designs of Wren and Handel, Canaletto's paintings created a remarkable synthesis of massiveness and delicacy, spaciousness and human warmth. With these three creators we reach the culmination of the Southern baroque manner.

*T*hus far the baroque manner has been dealt with primarily as the creation of the Italians which spread northward from the Italian peninsula. It is necessary also to consider an area which remained largely untouched by Southern developments, the Germanic North. It is true that many Northern artists came directly under Italian influence: Dürer in the Renaissance, for example; the German composers Schütz and Handel in the baroque. To their number should also be added the Flemish painter Peter Paul Rubens, who fell under the influence of the Italian baroque early in the seventeenth century. Rubens' great admiration for both Michelangelo and Caravaggio is evident in his expansive, somewhat flamboyant canvases.

On the whole, however, the North retained a strong predilection for the artistic ideals of the late Gothic, especially its complexity, its pursuance of fantasy and distortion in order to achieve a sense of personal symbolism and mystery. Even in the paintings of Brueghel, dealing as they often do with folk subjects, we can readily detect lingering traces of Gothic unrealness. In his sharply outlined, often grotesque figures, Brueghel was the heir of an even earlier folk-mystic, Hieronymus Bosch, whose familiar *Garden of Delights*, from the turn of the sixteenth century, is a remarkable blend of naturalism with monsters and distorted beings. Gothic artists were seldom timid about mixing direct statement with involved metaphor.

The Gothic metaphor was hardly antiëmotional, however. Unreality in Bosch was directly allied with the expression of tortured inner sufferings. This is clearly seen in the few surviving paintings of Bosch's younger contemporary, Mathias Grünewald. There is nothing exceptionally naturalistic about such a work as Grünewald's *Crucifixion* panel in the Eisenheim altarpiece; it is as though he had set aside any attempt at pictorial naturalness to create a study in pure emotion.

These Northern artists who remained untouched by Italian humanism continued in this metaphoric vein long after the feeble toehold of the Gothic manner in the South had vanished. Along with the persistence of symbolism and "secret" messages, Northern music also retained the fascination with complexity

138

and mathematical designs that was seen in the contrapuntal writings of Obrecht and other composers of the late fifteenth century. The gradual decline of counterpoint as the prevailing mode of musical composition, which eventually resulted in the birth of opera in Italy, did not take place among "pure" Northern composers. The Netherlandic contrapuntal manner had continued, refined and subtilized to be sure, among Germanic composers in the sixteenth century, and in the baroque era there occurred no radical break with counterpoint, no manifesto from a camerata, such as had taken place in Italy. Even those Germans who traveled to Italy in the early baroque and studied the new style there at first hand were unable to instill into the Northern public any desire for a break.

Heinrich Schütz, for example, brought the Italian operatic style to Germany and created there a repertory of sacred pieces in something like the Monteverdian manner. But late in life he, too, abandoned this style and composed two oratorios on the Passion very much in the manner of the earlier Flemish polyphony, for singing without instrumental accompaniment. In certain of his earlier vocal works, however, Schütz did establish a musical style which partook somewhat of the Italian manner, and which had considerable influence on his fellow Northerners. This was the "sacred concerto," a setting for voices, chorus, and instruments of a sacred text in German—either a scriptural fragment or a free paraphrase thereof by a contemporary poet—that might be used as part of the Lutheran service. The form came to be called *cantata*, literally "something sung" but connotatively "something sacred sung."

The mainstay of the Lutheran service was the chorale, the short, hymnlike melody with simple harmonization which Luther had devised as a way of reaching the congregation. The cantata of the middle baroque in Germany was the first attempt to expand the significance of the chorale by making it serve a larger musical form. In the typical cantata the chorale melody is worked into one or all of the sections contrapuntally, while the text is usually a free paraphrase on the words of the particular chorale employed. The freely composed sections of the cantata, which might include arias, choruses, short

139

recitatives, and instrumental interludes, share to some degree the sturdy, simple melodic nature of the chorale itself. Although Schütz introduced some Italianism into his sacred pieces, he never abandoned completely in these works the simpler, more foursquare Germanic melody, nor did his successors, who include such names as Franz Tunder, Mathias Weckmann, and Dietrich Buxtehude.

The chorale was central to a great deal of Northern baroque instrumental music as well. In one of the most important forms developed in the mid-seventeenth century, the *chorale-prelude*, the organist worked the melody into any number of various contrapuntal treatments, or used it as the basis of a series of variations.

The chorale-prelude and the theme with variations were among the major instrumental forms; standing above them as the prime mode of musical thought for composers in the North was the *fugue*. Wide-ranging and complex, this style had grown clearly out of Renaissance contrapuntal practices, and had been attempted in the South by Frescobaldi and others.

The direct antecedent of the fugue was the ricercare, which has already been noted in connection with the works of Frescobaldi as the instrumental counterpart of Palestrina-style sacred polyphony. It was prevailingly serious in tone, and given over to the imitative working out of a short melodic subject among several voices. The ricercare, or its close relative the *fantasia*, was developed in the early baroque by the Netherlandic composer Jan Sweelinck, whose work marks the final stage of two centuries of glorious musical achievement by composers of the Lowlands. In Sweelinck's famous *Chromatic Fantasia*, the initial theme, which is of an intensely chromatic and somber character, is played against itself and against newly introduced melodic ideas. It also occurs from time to time rhythmically altered, or played twice as fast or twice as slow. In all, this magnificent work of eight minutes' duration is really an early example of the fugue, and a remarkably well-developed one. It is complex and almost mystically poignant in its powerful use of dissonance.

From Sweelinck to Bach the history of the Northern baroque is to a large

Vermeer's Lady at Virginal, like many of his paintings, is peopled with figures of artistic sensitivity and incorporates geometric patterning. Serene yet compelling, it reflects the cool, reserved aesthetic of the North.

141

extent one of growing mastery over the handling of fugal techniques, and
the permeation of these techniques into all manner of composition, vocal as
well as instrumental. Other contrapuntal forms also flourished, though to a
lesser degree. Principally these were the passacaglia and chaconne, characterized by a repeated short bass figure.

Among the noncontrapuntal instrumental forms of the North, the *suite*
held primary importance. These were sets of stylized dance movements which,
like the concerti grossi and sonatas of Corelli, were planned as much more
than movements collected at random. The various sections were unified by
being in the same key, but contrast was achieved by following a slow dance

143

with faster movement. Suites were created for solo keyboard, or for groups of strings or bass.

This, then, was the diversity of music in the Northern countries around 1680. Native opera had not gained a foothold to any great extent, although there were performances of the Roman and Neapolitan repertory in ducal courts in Germany and Austria. The success of the Italian school of string players also led to the establishment of string orchestras in several palaces, but they too began life with imported repertory, rather than German-composed works. The major efforts of the Germans were expended in the service of the Lutheran church, or in creating contrapuntal music to be played by musicians in the employ of noble patrons.

Intellectual as its appeal may have been (as opposed to the crowd-pleasing music of the South), the German baroque repertory had its own attractions. It was a turbulent, restless music, far more so than the platitudinous operas of Rome and Naples at their banal norm. It allowed for a high degree of fantasy. Heinrich Biber's sonatas for violin and basso continuo, many of them written in conformity with the contrapuntal practices of the time, nevertheless bore descriptive titles and purported to illustrate Biblical and other sacred stories. Johann Kuhnau's *Biblical Sonatas* for harpsichord were similarly descriptive: the "thrrrrp" on the harpsichord as David flings the stone at Goliath is a moment of great charm. Even Bach indulged in this kind of writing at least once. His harpsichord *Capriccio on the Departure of A Beloved Brother* calls at one point for the player to imitate the sound of coach horns as the brother sets out on a journey, and ends with a fugue on the coachman's song.

Contrapuntal intricacy, passion, and fantasy—there was little in Northern baroque music of the late-baroque Italian serenity. It was a musical language of intense chromaticism and dissonance. Composers underlined words of particular emotion in the cantatas with especially strong dissonant chords, enhanced often with striking instrumental coloration. Compared to the grand, vast expanse of Italian music, or to the works created for the French court of Louis XIV, the Northern music was introspective, even brooding.

144

*R*embrandt, too,
was deeply impressed by
the possibilities of
dim, mysterious lighting.
Understated,
almost flickering gold
in *Man With
the Golden Helmet*
recalls mystical
harmonies and sudden,
harrowing modulations
of such a piece
as the ''Crucifixus'' from
Bach's Mass in B minor.

145

A synthesis of a sort does become apparent in Northern art by the middle of the seventeenth century—not necessarily between the Gothic ideal and Italy, as was the case with Dürer and Schütz—but between the Gothic ideal and its own milieu. This synthesis is clearly seen in the works of three indigenous geniuses of the late Northern baroque, the painters Rembrandt and Vermeer and, a generation later, the composer Johann Sebastian Bach.

Rembrandt was influenced to some extent by Italian painters, but primarily by the most "Gothic" of the mannerists, Caravaggio. Rembrandt's supreme mastery over color and light, especially his mystical, dark hues, and the subtle, somber luminescence that radiates from such paintings as *Man with a Golden Helmet*, resembles but surpasses the Caravaggio idiom. However, Rembrandt's magnificence lies in his mysticism, the brooding, unspoken passion of his portraits, the tragic overtones of his religious paintings, the deep humanness of his every creation.

Rembrandt, in his power to project onto a painting his personal relationship to his subject, exemplified the continuing tone of Gothicism in the Northern baroque. He expressed through his use of color and the tension that infuses his composition, a point of view that remains his own secret. It is not given the viewer to understand. Rembrandt is, if anyone was, a metaphysical painter.

In the paintings of Vermeer we see another side of the persistent Gothicism. These, too, the artist infused with a degree of personal fantasy. He also gave them his own unique quality of charm. His Northernness shows primarily in his passion for exact mathematical designs, his love of geometrical patterns (tiled floors, for example), and the way he uses a strong sense of design in communicating deep emotion. This, too, can be said of the works of Bach.

Among important creators of the late Northern baroque, the name of the Viennese architect Fischer von Erlach must not be omitted. In many of his great buildings for Vienna, notably the Karlskirche, von Erlach clearly belongs to the classic revival that has already been noted in England in the works of Christopher Wren. But there is another side to Fischer's work that reflects

146

the era's lingering Gothicism. It can be seen in his Holy Trinity Monument in Vienna, a work of intense inwardness that seems to revolve desperately around its axis, as though seeking to strangle itself. The tension of such a creation comes about through what would be described musically as counterpoint overlaid with dissonance, highly complex, but not without an immense, controlling order.

It seems too much to ask that the music of one man should embody all rich and diverse artistic ideals of the late Northern baroque, yet this was the achievement of Johann Sebastian Bach. In a sense, Bach was a provincial composer, rather uninterested in the musical currents around him. Yet he knew Italian music well enough to work with great fluency in the realm of the concerto. He was familiar enough with the dance music of France to essay with great success sets of suites in the French manner for violin, solo harpsichord, and full orchestral ensemble.

But he was primarily a composer in the service of the church, and the Lutheran chorale remained central to his musical thinking. It forms the basis for his more than two hundred church cantatas and is treated therein in every possible contrapuntal fashion. Just to read through the way Bach harmonized these melodies, usually in a straightforward and unadorned manner, is to sense the hand of a creator as sensitive to the power of harmony as Rembrandt was to color.

Bach invented nothing. He worked in the forms common to all composers of his time and locality but with better results. He made transcriptions for keyboard solo of some of the Vivaldi string concertos, in most cases evolving a taut and concise design superior to the original. His six Brandenburg Concertos are exercises in the Corelli plan of the concerto grosso, mingling dance-like movements, fugues, and purely abstract musical designs, and ennobling the medium immeasurably by virtue of his remarkable scoring and the unadorned humanness of his expressivity.

Often the complexity of his designs is overwhelming. The opening chorus of the Passion Oratorio according to Matthew is a huge contrapuntal concep-

148

tion involving intricate antiphonal effects between two choruses and two orchestras, in the old Venetian-Roman manner. These are joined by a third element, a chorus of treble voices which intones a chorale melody that is then worked into the already intricate texture. In another work he takes a slow movement from a keyboard concerto—in itself an elaborate and completely worked out passacaglia—adds four new choral parts, and makes it serve as the first chorus of a cantata (No. 146).

For all the monumentality of his grandest designs, there is also a serene, seraphic side to his music that is somewhat less famous. At times the figurations in his contrapuntal designs are jagged and tense, like streaks of lightning: the chaconne for unaccompanied violin, for example, or the passionate opening of the B Minor Mass. But at other times he works with musical ideas so delicate, so quietly haunting that the breath all but stops: the opening chorus of the Cantata No. 8, or the chorale-prelude on *Wachet auf.*

Given his harmonic sense and mastery of the most intricate convolutions of the contrapuntal style, Bach created a repertory of music that epitomizes the highest ideals of the baroque manner. A great Bach fugue has in it the same coiled-spring tension that we find in the David of Michelangelo. His brilliant choral movements, with their dazzling instrumental halo of trumpet peals and percussion—the Gloria of the Mass, for example—have the spaciousness of a Bernini design. The instrumental and orchestral concertos have an emotional balance that reflects the classicism of the late baroque throughout Europe. It is for these reasons that Bach stands as the culminating figure of baroque art.

A vastly different kind of artistic expression was already taking shape during Bach's lifetime. His sons—the many of them who became important composers—rejected almost totally the ideals their father's music had embodied. His music remained obscure for nearly a century after his death, sought out only by a few connoisseurs. But among these were Mozart and Beethoven, who, although themselves steeped in far different artistic currents, recognized immediately the stature of the Leipzig choirmaster and found that he had much to teach them.

8. The Rise

of Romanticism

Until quite recently, popular attitudes divided the realm of serious music into two major divisions: prehistoric and historic. The dividing date was the sixth decade of the eighteenth century, the point we have now reached. Bach died in 1750; Handel, in 1759. Until the advent of the long-playing record, access even to the major works of these supreme masters was difficult and spotty. In 1948 there were fewer than half a dozen cantatas of Bach that could be heard in the home. Now more than half of his two hundred works in this form have been recorded. Vivaldi was an unknown, and so were most of the operas and oratorios of Handel. As for music from before their time, the little that could be found on records, or heard in concert, was usually so mangled and romanticized as to be far removed from the original.

There was some justification for applying this dividing date to the musical repertory. A major revolution did take place in music around 1750, not so much in the nature of the art itself as in its place in society.

For all the splendor of the great works composed before this time, it was nonetheless clear that music occupied a place in public favor somewhat secondary to the arts of painting, architecture, and sculpture. It served as an adjunct to religious observance, or as an adornment to the noble or royal life in the palaces of the mighty. What little music there was for direct public consumption—the operas in large Italian cities, for example—was generally of a quality far below the best of its time.

The most significant thing about music from 1750 on, therefore, is that it is public, as were the cathedrals and great buildings of the past and the art works they contained. Consequently, music became increasingly important in people's lives. For this reason—among many others—the prestige of music, relative to the other arts, increased markedly.

There were clear causative factors for the lessening of prestige among the visual arts. The church seemed no longer to have the interest or ability to support the great building program that had gone on from the time of Charlemagne until the end of the baroque. The nobility declined in wealth and power, and could no longer erect and decorate new palaces with the splendor of Chambord or Versailles. Among the individuals affected by this decline were the artists. A painter, sculptor, or architect earns his support with each art work as it is turned out, and so he lives from work to work; a composer, like a playwright, can sell tickets and obtain publishers, thereby reaping a continued harvest.

Thus, the composer in the late eighteenth century became a free agent, with all the paraphernalia needed to keep his art before the public: traveling virtuoso performers, orchestras, municipal opera companies, even music critics. (The profession of music criticism, whose worthy aim was to serve as intermediary between the creators of music and the readers of newspapers and magazines who were to support those creators, came into being around 1720 in the person of Johann Mattheson of Hamburg. Significantly, he seemed almost unaware of the existence of Johann Sebastian Bach.)

The revolution in public tastes occurred gradually. France, in particular, held to the earlier tradition of the arts as the property of the aristocracy, relinquishing this hold only late in the century, long after the public had gained access in Italy, Germany, and England. French painting remained elegant and reserved. François Boucher filled his canvases and panels with allegories in which exquisite detail cut off all direct emotional communciation. He and his confrères, Jean Honoré Fragonard and Antoine Watteau, created a shimmering world of lights, shades, and colors in which elegant ladies frolicked gaily at garden parties as gallant gentlemen stood decorously by. Any hint of eroticism was portrayed with so light a heart as to make unthinkable any deeper implication.

This was the art known as *rococo*, a composite French term derived from *roche* and *coquille* (rock and shell), thus describing a manner of decoration in which bits and pieces of naturalistic forms are brought together. It had its musical counterpart in the fanciful pieces for harpsichord by François Couperin and Jean Philippe Rameau in which the chief source of propulsion was the intricate ornamentation of practically every principal note in the melody. The music itself was mainly dance-derived, but the glittering succession of

*O*pening pages: Fragonard's *The Lover Crowned,* with its air of languor and wit, its allegorical conceits, and its wash of elegant decoration, brings to mind fanciful pieces for harpsichord composed at the time by Rameau and Couperin. Above: Sketch of flautist by Watteau.

153

trills, turns, and grace notes provided a fantastic cloud that all but obscured the basic rhythmic scheme.

This music is not without emotion, but it is held in check by a strong sense of reason and balance. It is achieved by the delicate languor of melody, subtly tinted by a refined and imaginative harmonic style. This emotion springs from a wealth of detail and color lying on the surface, readily accessible to the listener. It is not imbedded in structure and texture, as with the music of Bach, nor arrived at through grand overstatement as in the Italian operas of the late baroque or the oratorios of Handel.

The new spirit which came into music in the eighteenth century was simply this: to achieve communication primarily through a line of melody and its surrounding color. To this kind of art the most applicable term is *romantic*, since the primary object is a direct appeal to the emotions. Rameau himself made a vital contribution to the new age in his important *Treatise on Harmony*, which served to codify current attitudes toward the way the vocabulary of musical coloration might be used. The treatise (by implication,

155

at any rate) established the dominance of the melodic line with harmonic support over the contrapuntal techniques of the Renaissance-baroque.

Actually, of course, this kind of thinking had been in effect for some time, especially in Italy. Italian composers at the beginning of the baroque had abjured counterpoint as antidramatic, and the violin concertos and Neapolitan arias of the late baroque had also stressed medolic line as the highest musical ideal. The revolution of the musical rococo, then, was in part the permeation of Northern music by Italian ideals, and the supplanting by these ideals of the complex, tense intellectualism which observers chose to find in the few works of Bach known at the time.

But the Italian style of the late baroque was enmeshed in a complexity of its own. The cult of the virtuoso had nourished a dense and meaningless tangle of decorative notes around the musical line; opera had become an artificial and overloaded art, far removed from the dramatic directness of Monteverdi. The public, at least the intelligent segment of it, was ready for something with greater meaning. Rameau himself achieved this in his own operas, lavish in their stage requirements, but with a vocal style in which the gracefully simple lines were much more in tune with dramatic situations than they were in typical Italian works of the period. What is even more striking in Rameau's operas is that the orchestra, which in Italy had been pared down to allow the singers full command of the scene, was greatly augmented and given a far more important role in creating the mood.

Rameau left no direct musical successors, but his own operatic ideals continued in force. In England the protest against the ornate Italian style, as typified there in the operas of Handel, took the form of *Beggar's Opera*, a brilliant satire by Christoph Pepusch, to a text by John Gay. It worked within the framework of grand opera but substituted folk songs or folklike music for the elaborate and stereotyped arias, and a story of lowlife characters in London for Handel's gods and shepherds. The "opera" was fantastically successful with the public, and imitations by the hundreds were done in England and Germany.

*A*ngels, cupids, birds, and jewels surround "Venus at Her Toilette" in this elaborate canvas by Boucher. Here is the same fanciful spirit that gave rise to ornate, artificial, but strangely touching music of French rococo.

156

The great philosopher, aesthetician, and encyclopedist Jean Jacques Rousseau continued the battle in France with his one important attempt at composition, the short opera *Le Devin du Village (The Village Soothsayer)*, in which the simple, rustic characters enact their little adventure in music of a disarming sweetness and naturalness. And in Italy there was Giovanni Pergolesi's *La Serva Padrona* which, like its Northern counterparts, forswore ornate and complex vocal paraphernalia for tuneful and unadorned melodic phrases.

All these works had an enormous appeal because they dealt with simple human beings depicted musically in simple ways. Lines, both dramatic and musical, were cleanly drawn and uncluttered. Furthermore, these compositions were all comedies. The operatic public, wearied by the problems of mythological and historical personages, could now relax in the presence of opera, be reached by recognizable and hummable tunes, and come out refreshed, if not uplifted.

But the new simplicity could be made to work in a more serious context as well. The Viennese composer Christoph Gluck, after turning out a number

159

Ballet and
opera in France remained
the province of the
aristocracy. Thus, in
performance of
Gluck's *Il Parnasso,* as
painted by Greipel,
there is elegance on
both sides of the curtain.

of respectable imitations of the grand Italian manner, made, in 1762, a series of new decisions about the physiognomy of the serious opera. Significantly, his first "reform" opera was, like the first Italian operas of the baroque, a setting of the story of the supreme musician, Orpheus.

In this score Gluck stripped away much of the antidramatic trappings that had grown around opera in the century and a half since Monteverdi's *L'Orfeo.* He loosened the formalized structure that had isolated the action (recitative) from the contemplation (aria) in favor of a more continually flowing vocal line. He ruled out the singers' prerogative of adding improvised coloratura and cadenzas in favor of a simple and unadorned melody closely related to the mood of the text. He increased the roles of the chorus and orchestra, using the latter brilliantly to suggest the atmosphere of each scene. In short, he re-created the dramatic urgency of Monteverdi, while working with the more regular, harmonically simpler style of his own time.

The age of the rococo had begun in profuse ornamentation but had moved rapidly toward stark simplicity. Again, as so often in the past, this new impulse toward clarity and balance was part of a general surge toward classicism. European architecture was again in thralldom to revived Greek and Roman models. The pillared façade became an obsession. Jacques Soufflot brought it to Paris in his Panthéon begun in 1754. England, which had seen the beginnings of the new classicism in Christopher Wren's churches, witnessed later manifestations in London's Chiswick and Somerset Houses. Thomas Jefferson designed his home at Monticello out of a desire to transplant Rome's designs to the Virginia countryside. This was the time of extensive excavations throughout the ancient world, led by the archaeologist and art historian Joachim Winckelmann, whose discoveries made him as popular as if he himself had built the Roman Forum.

The neoclassic impulse also was nurtured from an unexpected source. An increase of trade between Europe and the Orient had resulted in a mania for certain of the elements found in Eastern art. *Chinoiserie* was everywhere, and in its aspect of serenity it oddly mirrored the new classic ideals. A blending

of the two can be seen, for example, in the vases and plates of Josiah Wedgwood: Greco-Roman in shape and ornamentation, but with color schemes, as the familiar blue-and-white, that recalled the Orient.

Sculptors, too, found in the latest classic revival a justification for aiming their own sights at Greek and Roman models. Jean Antoine Houdon's statue of George Washington, although clothed in the statesman's garb of the 1780's rather than the toga, is the artist's attempt to create an American Caesar Augustus. Antonio Canova's study of Pauline Borghese as Venus could have been excavated on an Athens hillside.

However, to think of the late eighteenth century as purely a classic age is to overlook a great deal. Many music historians tend to do so, finding irrefutable justification in the clarity of Gluck's operas and, as we shall soon see, in structural practices among composers of instrumental music. Certainly, also, the age of reason and enlightenment as proclaimed by Rousseau and the French Encyclopedists, with their clarion call for a return to nature and naturalness, tempts one to regard 1750 as the beginning of a new Renaissance founded upon the exercise of reason.

But the era also bred its own restlessness, a new pathos opposed to the ethos of the Paris Panthéon. It was sounded in Germany by Gotthold Lessing, who based his great essay on aesthetics on the straining, surging, rediscovered Laocoön sculpture of the late Greek civilization. It was present in the massiveness and heroism of Schiller's dramas and in the poignant lyrics of Goethe. It was in the concern with demonism of a minor but interesting school of German painters that flourished around 1780—in the beasties of John Henry Fuseli's *The Nightmare* that swirl above a tortured maiden.

This was the *Sturm und Drang* (storm and stress) in which poets, dramatists, and painters rebelled against the formalism of the latest classic revival, giving the lie to the overall depiction of the times as classic and restrained.

The musical style of the time was formed by a blend of romantic restlessness and a serenity that might be called classic. The second element derived from Italian opera, which by that time had greatly simplified its musical lan-

163

guage. The trend toward simplicity continued well into the eighteenth century, and formed the basis, not only of operatic thinking, but of much thinking in instrumental composition as well. It provided composers with a melodic vocabulary far different from that of the baroque, a style that was tuneful and immediate, shapely and symmetrical. A Bach melody, any one you might choose, is shaped roughly like a spiral. It works its way upward, seemingly capable of infinite expansion. A classic melody—take, for example, the famous Minuet in the Elysian Fields ballet in Gluck's *Orpheus*—moves instead in short, regular phrases, a movement upward balanced immediately by a return downward. It is a classic shape: a pediment perhaps, supported on evenly spaced harmonic pillars.

The new operatic style contributed to the great movement that swept through musical Europe around 1750—the establishment of the orchestra as the most important performing unit. Following the example set by the Italians late in the previous century, noble houses throughout the continent established and maintained ensembles of up to fifty resident musicians, strings mostly, but also

164

wind and brass players. The symphonic sound as we recognize it today began to take shape.

It was a homogeneous sound. Whereas earlier the orchestral instruments were treated soloistically, each section with its own part, the new orchestra had a different orientation. The main emphasis was now upon the strings, with the songlike melodies carried principally by violins supported by the lower members of the string choir. Additional color was provided by sustained chords from the winds: flute, oboe, bassoon, and the newly invented clarinet. Reinforcement at climactic passages came from trumpets, horns, and kettledrums.

It would be well at this point to pause and consider briefly the actual nature of the harmonic and melodic style that permeated eighteenth-century orchestral music.

Harmony is simply the relationship between notes heard simultaneously. It is heard, or at least analyzed, relative to some series of standards. The ear hears certain sounds and combinations as harmonious, and others as nonharmonious or dissonant. A composer uses this interrelation of harmoniousness and dissonance to propel his music on its course.

The quality of being harmonious exists when a harmony is clearly related to its key, or tonality. Thus, if we are in the key of C major (obtained on the piano by playing only the white notes), any note not in that key (a black note) would be dissonant. Furthermore, there are certain notes within that key which are, so to speak, the pillars on which its harmony is built. These are the three notes which form the tonic chord. In the key of C they would be the notes C, E, and G.

The clarity of the typical "classical" melody comes from its close adherence to the notes of the tonic chord, or to simple scale passages which also strongly define the key. The slow movement of Haydn's *Surprise* Symphony, for example, is in C major, and the opening notes of the melody are C-C-E-E-G-G-E, an emphatic definition of that tonality. On the other hand, the opening of Beethoven's *Eroica* Symphony, although it begins with the chordal notes of its particular tonality, immediately veers off to a note which does not belong

to the key at all, establishing a dissonance and its concomitant feeling of drama.

Two great musical forms were developed to occupy the attention of the orchestra. One was the *symphony*, a work in three or four contrasting sections set apart by speed and mood but unified by beginning and ending in the same key. The other was the *concerto*, the outgrowth of the baroque form in which a solo instrument was pitted against the orchestra in a kind of dramatic conversation, and in which the soloist was expected to perform with a degree of virtuosity comparable to the singer in an opera. The bulk of the concerto writing was for violin or some other melody-carrying instrument, like the flute. But another new instrument was coming into vogue as well, with great expressive qualities despite its basically percussive nature, and composers were all agog over this newcomer, the *pianoforte*, so named because of its ability to play both soft *(piano)* and loud *(forte)*.

Germany was the principal center for orchestral composition, and the orchestras at Berlin and Mannheim were famed for their virtuosity and especially for an ability highly prized at the time: to be able to shade the volume of sound from the merest whisper to the mightiest roar. Mannheim, especially, became an important musical center attracting composers not only from Germany, but also from Bohemia and Poland.

The "Mannheim style," in fact, became the clearest foreshadowing of growing orchestral importance. Johann Stamitz, a Bohemian who founded the orchestra there under the patronage of the Elector Duke Carl Theodor, is the man generally conceded to be the true "father of the symphony."

The broad outlines of the symphony reflect in the clearest possible way the ideals of classicism, although the language itself allowed for great tension. Orderly, controlled contrast is at the core. The movements of the symphony contrast among themselves in pace and to a certain extent in mood, yet they are unified by key and by other considerations of mood. If a symphony begins brilliantly and in a festive manner, it will round out its journey in time by returning to this outlook at the end, even though intervening movements may introduce a contrasting note of contemplation.

Co-existing with classicists was a small group of painters and musicians whose mysterious works were conditioned by a revival of interest in haunted tales of folklore. Fuseli's *The Nightmare* is an example of this *"Sturm und Drang."*

167

Likewise, the shape within individual movements contains these same interlinked ideals of unity and contrast. The design of the first movement is usually the most elaborate. A theme is stated, and this also serves to emphasize the key of the movement. Then there is a harmonic movement away from that key, a period of unrest following a period of repose, until finally there is a closing-off in a new key, usually emphasized by new themes. Then follows an even longer period of unrest, in which elements already heard may be stated again, broken apart or otherwise "developed." This period of unrest has as its goal a building up of tension which is relieved by the return of the initial material in the original key, and the movement is concluded by a recapitulation of most of the original material, but this time all in the basic key. Thus, the first-movement form fundamentally consists of three major sections: exposition, development, and recapitulation. Framing these there may be, at the option of the composer, a slower introduction and a final peroration, or *coda*. It is a beautiful, logical pattern, one which preserves certain set outlines and yet provides for infinite variety of treatment.

Basically, this first-movement form (or "sonata form," to give it its customary name) is an extension of the baroque shape we have already encountered within the movements of a Corelli concerto, or in the sonatas of Domenico Scarlatti. What is different in the eighteenth century is the breadth of the form, and especially the complete recapitulation. The Scarlatti plan honored the idea of departure from the basic key and a return to it, and also of contrast between periods of harmonic stability and unrest, but the late-eighteenth-century composer makes his points more emphatically by enhancing each new section with new thematic material.

The other movements of the symphony were usually, but not always, simpler in construction. The slow movement was often in sonata form, but could also take the form of a theme and variations, or of a simple three-part shape: an idea, a contrasting idea, and a return to the original. The third movement was usually a contrastingly lighter section, most likely a minuet or some other dance, again in three-part form with the contrasting middle section often

168

more lyrical and flowing. Frequently the symphony consisted of just these three movements, but sometimes there was· also a brilliant finale. This might be in sonata form, but more often took the form of a *rondo*, an alternation of a principal idea and several contrasting ideas. The finale tended to be short and brilliant, without the complex working-out of material characteristic of the first movement.

The symphonic form was also the basis of the other instrumental forms of the time. In the concerto a soloist was added to the orchestral fabric, and his appearance often was delayed by an orchestral introduction which served to build tension. This opening *ritornello* usually went through some or all of the material out of which the ensuing sonata-form movement was to be constructed. To satisfy the demands of the soloist, there was usually a place near the end of each movement for a cadenza, a free, virtuosic improvisation.

Although the growth of the orchestral repertory is, for us, the most spectacular achievement of the late eighteenth century, there was also a considerable amount of activity in musical forms for fewer instruments. The pianoforte became enormously popular within a few decades after its invention in Italy. It was a smaller, less sonorous instrument than our modern concert grand, but its expressive possibilities were not lost on composers of the time. Carl Philipp Emanuel Bach, one of Johann Sebastian's sons who was musically active and important, was from all accounts a spectacular piano virtuoso and his large-scale piano sonatas are brilliant. They follow the form of the symphony: several movements, arranged as in the large-scale orchestral compositions.

This period also saw the rise of chamber music as an important and independent medium. If the symphony and concerto were the music for the large halls, the works for smaller groups—strings, strings and winds, strings and piano, indeed any conceivable combination—were suited for smaller gatherings, formal and informal. A ducal orchestra was also expected to have a ducal string quartet, or an ensemble of wind players, to provide background music at a banquet or garden party, and the composers of the time developed a large repertory of chamber works to suit such occasions.

Actually, the chamber repertory developed along two separate paths. On the one hand, the intimate surroundings of a small room brought intelligent listeners closer to the music, and encouraged in chamber music a subtlety and intellectual level not so feasible in the grander orchestral style. On the other, the incidental function of chamber music as background for dining or conversation brought about a lighter, less demanding style applied to a large number of short, uncomplicated movements that were in reality tunes strung together in a relatively loose organization: the *serenade, divertimento, cassation,* etc.

From the preceding discussion of formal practices among composers of the middle and late eighteenth century, it is clear that these artists hardly deserve the label of superficiality that is commonly ascribed to them.

Certainly, one could say that the simplicity of the new style, with its emphasis on melody and on slowly changing harmonies, was far removed from the deep intensity of the works of J. S. Bach. But this is not to say that the contrast was one between shallowness and high seriousness. Actually the spirit of the classical era took clear account of the power of music to touch the emotions. And while composers seemed almost obsessed with the method of classical organization, it can be seen in retrospect that their intent in using classical form was to attain control over emotional expression, not to silence it.

*R*ich in tonal possibilities, one of Cristofori's early pianofortes (1720) was to usher in a new sound in music, and ultimately a new aesthetic as well.

9. Twilight of Classicism

Supreme artistic creators do not belong to one single historic moment. Nor do they embody a single artistic trait. Michelangelo, product of the humanist ideals of the Renaissance, brought to his art an urgency that imposes dynamism upon classic outlines. Monteverdi, sublime creator in a new musical realm, brought to opera the techniques and attitudes of the past in order to broaden its horizons and strengthen its purpose. Bach, crowning figure of the Northern musical baroque, enriched his language with ideas from Italy, his artistic antipode.

Joseph Haydn, Wolfgang Amadeus Mozart, and Ludwig van Beethoven were born within four decades of each other in German-oriented central Europe. Their mature musical life was centered around Vienna, where Franz Schubert also lived and died. It is common practice to think of the first two composers as bringing to a culmination the classic era in music, Beethoven as the bridge to romanticism, and Schubert as the first great romantic composer. Actually, it makes somewhat better sense to regard each of the four composers as embodying to some degree, throughout his musical lifetime, a dynamic balance between the two poles. But classicism was ebbing. By the end of the ninety-six-year span between the birth of Haydn in 1732 and the death of Schubert in 1828, the flame of musical classicism had been quenched.

The musical styles that had emerged late in the eighteenth century were of a uniformity that had seldom before existed in music. Both North and South were permeated with a kind of writing that stressed simple, symmetrical melodic construction, harmonic simplicity and a relatively slow rate of harmonic change, and a clear texture in which a single singing line floated upon its harmony with little inner contrapuntal activity.

Moreover, the organization of materials within a large-scale composition tended toward a certain set pattern, an orderly scheme of contrast between the principal key, or tonality, of a movement and a second related key. The little turbulence that occurred was in the passages of modulation, the change from one key to the contrasting one and the somewhat longer return to the original. It was a simple, affecting style, and in the hands of skillful composers

174

it was capable of creating a great deal of pleasure. Its successful practitioners were many. Among the Italians were Giovanni Battista Sammartini and Luigi Boccherini. In the North were several of the sons of Johann Sebastian Bach, particularly Carl Philipp Emanuel and Johann Christian, along with Johann Quantz, Michael Haydn (brother of Joseph), and Leopold Mozart (father of Wolfgang).

The operatic style of the time was no less simple. After a certain amount of bickering among the supporters of Gluck, Pergolesi, the old-fashioned Italian grand manner, and the folklike style typified by *Beggar's Opera*, an international style emerged which combined to some degree the strengths of all these types. From Pergolesi's *La Serva Padrona* there developed, in the hands of the Italians Domenico Cimarosa and Giovanni Paisiello, a comic-opera style that was tuneful and simple, with short, catchy arias and a graceful connecting recitative. From a certain reconciliation of the Gluck manner and that of the serious Italian opera, there grew a somewhat more cohesive serious style with an emphasis on long melodies of considerable poignance, and a simple and sentimental harmonic flow. The spawn of the *Beggar's Opera* was the German *singspiel*, which was comic, dealing usually with rustic characters; it had melodies in popular style and spoken dialogue instead of recitative. A close relative was the French *opéra comique*, in which the music was, again, extremely simple and the connecting dialogue was spoken.

The four composers mentioned at the start of this chapter were thoroughly trained from childhood in the styles of the eighteenth century. Each, in his own way, was to stamp upon a musical language strongly controlled by formula and cliché some special ennobling virtue from his own fund of imagination and insight. Each succeeded in this because he chose, rightly, to regard the standardized musical techniques of his time not as a rigid framework to be followed to the letter but as a general trend to be observed only in spirit. Within the general area of a classical framework, these men embodied a romantic, unbridled spirit, as had Michelangelo in his time two centuries previously.

Opening pages: Canova's statue of Pauline Borghese as Venus blends classic style with theatricality of sculptor's own time, in much the way that Haydn and Mozart "bent" classical formulas in music to accommodate their own expressive desires.

175

Haydn and Mozart were friends and colleagues, united by a strong and genuine regard for each other's music. "I assure you solemnly and as an honest man," Haydn once said to Leopold Mozart, "that I consider your son to be the greatest composer of whom I have ever heard." This remark was prompted by a series of string quartets which Mozart had dedicated out of love and friendship to his older colleague.

There were vast stylistic differences between the two composers, however, which cannot be explained simply. Although he wrote throughout his lifetime in every musical form of the time, Haydn was eminently an instrumental composer and his musical thinking came primarily from an insight into the dramatic potentialities of a solo instrument or an ensemble. Mozart, on the other hand, was drawn early in his life to the music of Italy, and his thinking in all his scores came primarily out of the language of opera, with its special range of musico-dramatic devices.

Haydn's great achievement was to bring to the symphony and its related forms a sense of dramatic urgency. He accomplished this in many ways. For one thing, he was a master of the sudden surprise—an abrupt change from loud to soft, a breaking-off in the midst of an idea to jump to a strange and distant key, a switch in sound from strings to winds or brass.

But even more important were his achievements in the realm of melody itself. Instead of the typical melody of his colleagues, fully formed, symmetrical, and usually constructed of simple scale-figures or arpeggios, Haydn devised a melody which was less serene, strongly rhythmic, composed of short, tense fragments which could be separated and rejoined differently to form still new ideas. Thus one feels in the course of a Haydn movement, especially a fast movement, that there is a constant process of expansion taking place, that the musical ideas stated at the beginning are only the initial glimpse of a much larger design. Furthermore, Haydn often uses these fragments, or motives, in a contrapuntal texture, thereby heightening the tension and increasing the dynamic detail.

This process of continual development of ideas, combined with his sense

176

of the dramatic use of instruments, gives Haydn's music a sweep and passion unknown in the works of other composers of his time. Even in his most light-hearted works there is a feeling of tension. This element allies Haydn to some extent with the *Sturm und Drang* poets; at the least, it is a departure from the purely classical spirit. Thus Haydn achieves an expansion of the orchestral language partly by incorporating into his style elements from the past. It is perfectly clear that the new orchestral style of the eighteenth century was born out of a desire to cleanse from music the complexities of old-fashioned contrapuntal methods. Yet Haydn, as Monteverdi before him, realized that purity of expression need not demand an entirely new beginning. He had access to a few of the works of J. S. Bach, and learned from them that there was a continuing validity in the old contrapuntal methods.

Mozart profited greatly from Haydn's example. From his Italian orientation he had developed ideas of his own about musical drama, but much of his unique manner of wringing the heart with music was gained through observation of Haydn's use of counterpoint. Like Haydn, Mozart could write melodies that carried the seeds of conflict. But with him the conflict was in the melody itself, not in its power to expand. A typical Mozart melody—the one which begins the *Jupiter* Symphony, for example—is made up of two distinct ideas set in a kind of question-and-answer form. This "conversational" construction is used in larger scale in many of his instrumental works. One senses it particularly in his mature piano concertos. In these there is a continuing dialogue between the solo instrument and the orchestra, and it is carried forward in such expressive musical language that the two voices seem ready to burst into words at any moment. Thus the idea of the concerto, which had been developed originally by Corelli and the northern Italians as an instrumental counterpart to the opera, and which had come to be regarded as a showpiece for the soloist's virtuosity, changed under Mozart to a far more subtle mode of expression.

But it was in opera itself that Mozart's particular genius blazed brightest. His major operatic works are comedies, influenced largely by the Italian

177

English portrait
artists of the late 18th century
worked in a style
that owed much to a number of
sources: to Flemish
baroque painters like Rembrandt,
to the same Italian
influences that shaped Rubens's
outlook, and—of course—
to their own English patrons. Both
Reynolds, in his portrait of
Lady Smith and Her Children (above),
and Gainsborough, in his
study of Lady Thicknesse (right),
display the same eclectic
flair one finds in the music composed
by Handel while in England.

178

forms as refined by Cimarosa. But Mozart's comedies are far from pure merriment. The humanity he gives to characters like Countess Almaviva in *The Marriage of Figaro*, or the jilted and betrayed ladies in *Don Giovanni*, elevates this music above the norm of the time. So also does Mozart's supreme sense of dramatic counterpoint. In his hands, not only are the arias a series of compelling musical portraits, but the ensembles become crucial to the unfolding of the plot.

This was a somewhat new concept. The bulk of Italian operatic writing consisted of arias for solo singers, plus an occasional chorus, plus a few moments in which two or more characters sang together. In Mozart, the ensemble becomes the climactic point of the action; he developed a remarkable instinct for setting a stageful of characters into simultaneous motion, each singing characteristic lines and words with running commentary from the orchestra, and all blending into a musically satisfying whole. In each of his three greatest Italian comedies—*The Marriage of Figaro, Don Giovanni*, and *Così fan Tutte* —all action seems to push toward resolution in an ensemble.

As their styles matured, both Haydn and Mozart used dramatic counterpoint with increasing importance. Haydn produced the remarkable final dozen of his symphonies on visits to London late in his career. Here he came into contact with the music of Handel and he returned to Vienna enthralled by the majestic late-baroque splendor of this music. It inspired him to write two magnificent oratorios, *The Creation* and *The Seasons*, both much in Handel's debt, yet both full of the special romantic warmth and wisdom that stems from Haydn's own kind of melodic writing, dramatic underscoring, and tone color.

Mozart discovered the music of Bach late in his own tragically shortened lifetime. Although his last great opera, *The Magic Flute*, is outwardly set in the light *singspiel* style with dialogue, there is also some of the baroque intensity of Bach's contrapuntal style to introduce a note of solemnity. And in the unfinished *Requiem*, his final work and one of great poignance, the urgency of Bach's manner is informed by Mozart's own kind of probing, human

179

melody, his innate feeling for the beauty of the eighteenth-century harmonic language at its freest.

That Haydn and Mozart accomplished their miracles within the outlines of classic form truly establishes the place of classicism in the artistic thinking of the late eighteenth century. Outwardly it was a time when adherence to classic models was probably more pervasive and less self-critical than at any other time of classic revival in artistic history. And yet, both composers succeeded in filling classic outlines with the passionate, the humorous, the colorful, the demoniac, in ways that were of their own invention and which belonged to no definable artistic movement.

Theirs is, then, a highly "impure" classicism, a formalism sullied purposely and brilliantly by romantic intrusions. And at the same time, similar "intrusions" were making strong inroads into other arts, as well.

We find evidence of this, for example, in the important English-American school of painters working about mid-century, Thomas Gainsborough and John Singleton Copley, most notably. The repose and classic organization of Gainsborough's portraits are constantly disturbed by a flicker of involvement, perhaps a haughty expression, a dramatic position of the subject's arm, or an explosive color. Copley has some of these mannerisms, too, in his formal portraits, but even more of the dramatic can be found in his remarkable *Watson and the Shark*, in which the grouping of tense figures in the small boat takes on some of the crowded, surging movement found in sculptured ensembles of the early baroque.

This dramatic quality appears even more compellingly in the work of another Englishman of the time, the mystic-poet-painter William Blake. In his remarkable book engravings, thunderbolts leap from on high in furious, swirling action-lines that kindle unmistakable recollections of Michelangelo. From a generation or more before Blake, the bitter, satiric engravings of William Hogarth show some of the same earthy observation and abrupt dramatic contrast that made the music of Haydn so popular in London.

On the continent, the conflict of classic and romantic permeated the broad

and spacious canvases of Jacques Louis David, painter-laureate to the Napoleonic regime but an even more interesting artist before that era. David's early leanings were strongly classic, but even in such a work as *The Death of Socrates* the strong play of lights and shadows imposes a Caravaggesque drama upon a basically classic grouping. And in his masterpiece, *The Assassination of Marat*, David works with a stark classic composition, almost like a frieze marble, but infuses into the classic proportions an overwhelming sense of personal involvement. If there is a Mozartian painting it is this, achieved two years after Mozart's death, full of the same irony and demonism that boils

181

*A*merican-born John Singleton Copley's *Watson and the Shark,* based on a true event, goes beyond the event to invest its subject matter with a mythic quality. It is in the vein of symbolism that was prevalent in Europe early in the Romantic era.

182

beneath the surface of *Don Giovanni*.

Significantly, no painter, sculptor, or architect of major significance was produced at this time by the German-speaking world, although its music, its poetry, and its drama were supreme. It would be another century and more before northern and central Europe yielded an artistic movement of the force and influence that the Dutch-German painters had maintained in the Renaissance and baroque.

The spirit of the age was in itself at odds with pure classicism. The French Revolution accustomed the public to a life punctuated with the grand, dramatic, romantic gesture. Patriotism came into the purview of the man in the street, and the excesses of the revolutionary years accustomed him to a life close to horror and public bloodshed as well. The need was everywhere apparent for artistic creation on a lavish scale, either in the space it should occupy or in the emotions it should depict, or both.

Thus the creators of the time bypassed Renaissance classic models in their search for inspiration in favor of the more passionate models from the Gothic or from the baroque. From this quest there came the fantastic tales of E. T. A. Hoffmann, with imagery reminiscent of the visions of Bosch. There arose also a passion among the reading public for a kind of stylized folk tale: the haunted, somber Scottish-Irish ballads of James Macpherson, allegedly taken from the ancient bard Ossian; the lyrics of *The Youth's Magic Horn*, purportedly the legends and outcries of central European rustics; the newly coined imitations by Goethe of the archaic folk ballad.

Painters, too, caught this new spirit: Eugène Delacroix, with his studies of bodies rotting in Hades or his savage, barbaric *Massacre at Chios;* Francisco Goya, with his blood-and-tear-stained depictions of the horrors of modern warfare. The spirit entered into opera as well, in the short-lived but popular "horror and rescue" musical dramas of the period 1790-1810. Here, Luigi Cherubini and François Le Sueur created huge, unsubtle, murky scores full of blood and thunder, with the ultimate rescue of the heroine brought about through the noble, patriotic dedication of the hero.

184

Beethoven's one opera, *Fidelio*, is this kind of work, and without question the best of its kind. For Beethoven's own passion, the ardor of his views on patriotism and heroism, his drive to operate with a language that could fill the huge spaces—all these were the products of the romanticism of 1800.

Returning from hearing a piano concerto by Mozart, Beethoven is said to have remarked to a friend: "Ah, we will never achieve that." And he was right. He was an entirely different sort of composer from Mozart. Where Mozart could express the most moving and intimate of human emotions through the power of a balanced melodic dialogue, subtly touched by poignant harmony, Beethoven leaned more toward Haydn's kind of writing, in which every idea seemed to strain at its framework to break into new ideas, to spin, develop, and expand.

A characteristic Beethoven idea is not a smooth melodic line but a co-agulation of nuggets. The opening theme of the Fifth Symphony is not, as many believe, a four-note motive of three eighths followed by a sustained half. It is a long, sweeping arch made up of that four-note motive stated, then restated, and then growing restlessly into a furious rat-a-tat of four-note figures. The opening of the Third Symphony (subtitled *Eroica*) is not a melody at all, but a simple arpeggio in E flat which peters out in harmonic un-certainty before it achieves completion. Not until the end of that movement, fifteen minutes later, do we hear this opening motif rounded off as a full melodic statement. And the course of the whole movement has been, in a very real sense, a struggle toward that rounding-off.

The *Eroica* has been described as one of the greatest single forward steps in the history of the arts. It is that for many reasons. Most obvious is its size, twice the length of any previous symphony. But the work's size is important only because of the way the outlines are filled. Beethoven fills in the fifty minutes of the *Eroica*, not by inventing twice as many melodies as Mozart or Haydn would, but by creating a limited number of ideas which explode to fill the space. Sometimes, as in the first and last movements, the process is a slow, inexorable growth which lifts the listener with it as it rises. At other

185

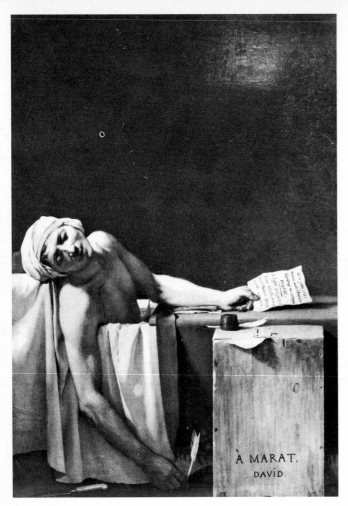

*P*aintings of Jacques
Louis David, like musical
compositions of his
time, are based on classic procedures
as point of departure;
thus, the sculptural quality in
depictions of great
pathos, such as *Marat Assassinated*
(above) and *The Death of
Socrates* (right).

186

times, as when the brass instruments in the slow movement begin a wordless scream on a single repeated note, one feels the fury as a sudden, blind eruption. This is probably what would be seen in Michelangelo's David if the sculptor had caught him a split second later. Because Beethoven, as a composer, works in time rather than in space, he makes explicit in his musical designs what the baroque or romantic painter and sculptor suggest is *about* to happen.

Not all of Beethoven's music is couched in the accents of fury and wild exultation that we find in the odd-numbered symphonies, the late string quartets, and the final piano sonatas. There was a mystical side to his work, as well, expressed in designs no less grand, but in accents quieter and more subtly colored. He had once envisioned writing an opera on *Macbeth* and while that project never materialized, there is music in one of his trios (for

189

piano, violin, and cello, Opus 70, No. 1) that was originally planned for the apparition scene. It has an unearthly quiet about it, a sense of half-muted mystery, that seems—no less than the extroverted passion of the *Eroica*—to suggest vast, solemn space. Only here the solemnity is enhanced by darkness.

That Beethoven accomplished this wide variety of mood within the standardized musical forms of classicism—sonata, rondo, theme and variations—is further testimonial to the validity of these musical designs themselves, and the flexibility with which imaginative composers could operate within them. Haydn and Beethoven could fill these forms with drama by unfolding imaginative and dynamic melody; Mozart could make the design serve as the stage for an unspoken human drama; all three composers could touch the heart, tickle the ribs, frighten, exhort, and cajole. Thus, abstract form born out of concern with structural consistency and symmetry became the vehicle for personal, and therefore nonabstract, communication.

Beethoven was not an innovator in the sense that Monteverdi had been, or Corelli. He was, like Bach, a man who expanded his own language within the accepted structural practices of the time. In his hands, as in those of Haydn and Mozart, the accepted formal designs of classicism had their outermost limits explored, while their outlines were respected.

In the generations that succeeded him, however, the outlines of classic form did indeed begin to disintegrate. Nineteenth-century romanticism sought other ideals. By 1830 the idea was abroad in Europe that the art of music should involve some sort of message, propounded through a unified musical design which broke with earlier ideas of contrast and symmetry.

Beethoven had tended strongly in that direction of unity. His Fifth Symphony is knit together by the aforementioned four-note motive, which recurs in some form in all four movements. In this work, too, the last two movements are no longer musically independent, but are connected by a transition passage. His Sixth Symphony is unified in another way. It is written to follow a program, the depiction of feelings experienced on being in the countryside. The Ninth Symphony is unified by the words of the solo bass

The romantic portraitist, as opposed to one of the preceding generation, tended to explore and exploit an emotional rapport between subject and artist, as did Schubert in his tender, intimate songs. This quality comes across strongly in Ingres's sketch for portrait of the Stamaty family.

191

Romantic artists—
painters and composers—
reacted more
strongly than ever to
the moods of their
world, to suffering,
triumph, sorrow, and
patriotism. Goya's *The
Second of May* is
charged with turmoil
of his native Spain
at time of
Napoleonic invasion.

voice in the finale, who begins by saying, "Oh, friends, let us no longer have these tones: let us, rather, raise our voices in song."

But in the works of another composer, almost contemporary with Beethoven, the idea of unified expression is even more clearly embodied. Franz Schubert's C major Fantasy for piano is outwardly a work in four separate movements, like the instrumental forms of the eighteenth century. Yet all four movements are musically linked. They proceed one to another without pause, and they all exploit a single melodic and rhythmic idea. The debt this *Wanderer* Fantasy owes to Beethoven's Fifth is obvious, but it goes several steps beyond.

Schubert's sovereign achievements, however, were in much smaller works. Goethe, Schiller, and a host of minor imitators had brought to a high polish the short lyric poem, in which the entire content is formed of a single strong emotion, expressed in as few words as possible. Schubert set these words to music, content not merely to decorate the words with a rising and falling musical line, but capturing in his music the mood of the poem itself. In this, also, the accompanying piano plays a vital part. As Mozart had done with the orchestra in his mature operas, Schubert brings the piano into equality with the voice, creating by its figurations and its harmony a musical mirror of the words.

Many influences shaped Schubert's extraordinary sense of melody. It partakes of the mellifluous, sentimental quality of Italian opera, or at least the finest in that language as distilled by Mozart. It is also strongly colored by the folk songs and dances of Austria and Germany. But mostly its quality is simply Schubert himself, an inexhaustible fountainhead of ideas with overwhelming emotional immediacy.

That Schubert's songs and short piano pieces are often sentimental there can be no doubt. The Vienna in which he was born and lived was a city where sentiment was cultivated, and a native could sense this perhaps more keenly than the immigrant Beethoven. A kind of decoration that has come to be known as Biedermeier was at the height of its vogue in Schubert's time: gim-

192

cracky, expansive, but lovably charming. Some of Schubert's songs reflect this style.

But the best of them, which means considerably more than half of the six hundred and three he wrote, are beyond question the closest that music has ever come to a complete union with poetry. That music could be so completely linked with another art, and that this union could, furthermore, so truthfully mirror the popular tastes of its time, was a progression toward the "total art work" envisioned not many decades later by Richard Wagner.

Schubert wrote in the larger forms as well. The spirit of eighteenth-century classicism hovers over his early symphonies and quartets, and, truth to tell, the young composer did not bring any special insights into his "solution" of the problems of classical form. His own brand of lyricism was somewhat at variance with the dramatic implications of the sonata form, which Beethoven had so keenly deciphered.

But in his last years Schubert did find a way of using large forms to the advantage of his particular gifts. He made the lyric sweep of his invention carry through the established points of musical articulation, blurring the outlines and retaining only the broadest aspects of the plan. His last symphonies—the *Unfinished* and the great C major—the sublime C major Quintet for strings, and the last three piano sonatas show a strength and a formal consistency that the earlier works lack.

But Schubert died tragically early, just as he had achieved this new step. He was one of the last major composers to whom classic form was of very great concern. In the period of high romanticism ways were found of loosening even further the strictures of formalism, to the point where content vastly overwhelmed shape. The germ of this new attitude was seen in Beethoven, who had been shown the way by Mozart and Haydn. It took root in the mature works of Schubert. And after Schubert it flourished mightily.

*I*ntelligentsia of Europe, awakening to the less-happy lot of the common people, met this theme in art of the 1800's, in works like Beethoven's opera *Fidelio* and in the searing caricature of Goya's *Pilgrimage to the Fountain of San Isidro.*

195

10. Flood Tide

of Romanticism

*T*raditionally, the term "romantic" has been reserved for the art of the nineteenth century, and this is valid if romanticism is understood in a restricted sense. In the most general sense romanticism can be defined as the personalization of art—the use of music, literature, and the visual arts to project the creator's own emotional reactions. By this criterion, the last century was most certainly a time of romanticism—but not the only time. Often in the history of art have the tides of personal expressivity inundated all consideration of abstract form and design.

Walter Pater wrote that all art aspires toward the condition of music. The nineteenth-century composer's viewpoint went even further. For him, music was the gathering together of all the arts. Richard Wagner sounded this concept most clearly, calling for a kind of music drama that would be the "total art work" (*Gesamtkunstwerk*), a synthesis of poetry, painting, sculpture, drama, and architecture, all under the dome of music. The concept was not entirely original with Wagner. Its inspiration came from the writing of earlier giants: Beethoven, with the tone-painting of his *Pastoral* Symphony and the embodiment of the heroic and demonic in the *Eroica* and the Fifth; Mozart, with his translation of human emotions into purely lyric terms; and Haydn, with his broad pictorialism in *The Seasons* and, in the mature symphonies, his startling use of orchestral effects.

The romantic era was a time of great contradictions in music. On the one hand, there was the idealization of instrumental music, which could now be made to express detailed scenic visions as well as abstract states of mind. On the other, there was the high regard given to the song and to the short piano piece, in which the exact wording of a lyric poem, expressed in words or implied instrumentally, directed the musical flow. The grand and the intimate were the twin goals.

In order to adapt the orchestral language to the demands of personal expression, it was necessary to rethink the grand plan of the classic design. Contrast and return were the broad principles of musical classicism, but a symphony which was to be about something could not easily be conceived along these lines. Composers solved this by blurring the architectural outlines, breaking down the points of articulation in favor of a smoother, more unified and homogeneous plan.

Hector Berlioz accomplished this in his *Fantastic* Symphony by threading through all five movements the story of a young man who takes opium in order to forget his unfaithful mistress and then has a series of visions in which she appears. "She" appears as a melody, an *idée fixe,* which occurs in one or another transformation in each movement.

Franz Liszt loosened the symphonic form still further, creating the *symphonic poem,* a work with a story line, whose sections usually contrasted in mood and pace but were united by an overriding theme which underwent transformations as the story progressed. The kind of musical unity hinted at by Beethoven in his Fifth Symphony and by Schubert in his *Wanderer* Fantasy now reached fruition.

To serve the composer's purpose in describing fanciful and emotional events, the orchestra itself became greatly expanded. More instruments were added to enrich the range of color, and the players themselves were required to execute feats of far greater virtuosity than composers had previously demanded. The range of sounds in Berlioz' compositions is truly fantastic. He learned to create an infinite variety of massive and delicate effects.

As the range of the orchestra was expanded, so also was the variety of musical devices available to the composer. There was an enormous expansion of the harmonic language in the nineteenth century. A particularly "juicy" chord could be used for its pure coloristic effect. Dissonance piled upon dissonance until the clear definition of the tonality of a composition was often in doubt for long minutes. This, coupled with the whole range of new orchestral sounds, created a music of great turbulence and unrest.

It was an age in which personal virtuosity and ostentation were highly prized. The flaming violinist Niccolo Paganini was not at all upset at the stories which circulated that he was in league with the devil, and he designed his own violin concertos to exploit fully his diabolical mastery of the instru-

The music of Chopin,
which depended for much of its effect
on the action of the piano's
pedal to create a harmonic blur,
is mirrored in such a
painting as this landscape by
Corot. Similarly, the
patriotism of his Polonaises reflects
the grand designs created by Rude
for Paris' *Arc de Triomph* (below).

ment. Franz Liszt, after devising his flamboyant and supertense orchestral manner, proceeded to make the solo piano the rival of the orchestra, with music that extracted from the keyboard the same measure of fire and brimstone of which the orchestra was capable.

Berlioz was not the concert virtuoso that Liszt and Paganini were, but the virtuosity in his conceptions was enough to qualify him for a place among the flamboyant romantics. The *Symphonie Fantastique* assures him this place, but even more grandiose was his *Grande Messe des Morts*, a Requiem created for a patriotic occasion in Paris, in which the depiction of the Day of Judgment

*W*hat Mendelssohn did
for the musical translation
of nature's mystery in
his *Hebrides* Overture, Turner
did on canvas (above)
in his *Lake of Lucerne.* The
other, epic side of
Mendelssohn, as in his *Elijah,*
is mirrored in such
Pre-Raphaelite painting as
Sir Edward Burne-Jones'
The Doom Fulfilled (right).

203

involves four separate groups of brass and percussion players, placed at the corners of the total performing body of orchestra and chorus, so that their fanfares and peals of thunder rolled across a wide space. Patriotism, along with personal suffering, elicited from the romantic composer an intense and high-strung musical expression. This work of Berlioz is the perfect complement in sound to the grandiloquent visual expressions of French nationalism common to the time, such works as the gaudy Napoleonic pageantry of the later David, François Rude's striving, shouting warrior group that depicts *La Marseillaise* in stone on the side of the Arc de Triomphe, and Delacroix's *Liberty Guiding the People.*

But there was a tender, more reasoned side to romantic expression, even on the epic level. The same Liszt who could draw the devil in white-hot orchestral tones in his *Faust* Symphony could also depict, in the same work, the tender innocence of Gretchen in the most delicate, haunting manner. And the same Berlioz who could send brass, percussion, and chorus thundering forth the Day of Wrath in the Requiem could also depict the Nativity in his oratorio, *L'Enfance du Christ*, in pastels of the most delicate evanescence.

The delicate, more intimate side of romanticism, with its emphasis on a quieter kind of mood-painting and a close identification with the lyric poets of the time, continued the small musical forms that had crystallized in the hands of Schubert. Robert Schumann's output of songs is, at its best, the near rival of Schubert's best. Schumann worked with a subtler, more mystery-tinged harmonic vocabulary. Sometimes, for example, a lyric that ended with a question would be set with a harmony that did not round itself off to a final cadence. Schumann also contributed to the literature a large repertory of fanciful, poetic piano pieces, often bearing fanciful and descriptive titles—*Butterflies, Colored Leaves, Forest Scenes*—and his mastery of a warm and richly colored piano style left its mark on his songwriting.

Schumann wrote for orchestra, too, but without the particular flair or flamboyance of Berlioz or Liszt. His symphonies do partake strongly of the romantic spirit, however. His *Rhenish* Symphony includes movements that

*I*n Courbet's *The Young Bather,* one is brought very close to the almost photographic reality of the situation depicted, the figure no less than the setting.

205

are short tone pictures of scenes along the Rhine, and his *Spring* Symphony is full of exuberant, if somewhat abstract, nature-painting.

But the supremely delicate tone painter of all the early romantic composers confined his efforts almost exclusively to the piano. In the veiled, atmospheric works of Frédéric Chopin one enters a new realm of piano sound. He used the pedal with more imagination and flexibility than ever before, and this, combined with long, wispy trails of gentle dissonances in the right hand, produced a tonal blur that creates the illusion of the piano as a lyrical, singing instrument. In this Chopin was clearly influenced by the Italian opera of the time, and his way of setting a long singing line over a gently undulating background for the left hand is, like the instrumental music of Mozart, an uncanny translation of operatic sentiment into purely instrumental terms.

The idea of the blur, whether applied to the outlines of a form, or to the sound itself, is a concept found everywhere in romantic art. Camille Corot, along with his French compatriots of the Barbizon School, revived the art of landscape painting with a technique that depicted not only the outlines of trees, the shoreline of a lake, or a small farmhouse in the distance, but washed over them the haze and the softness of light found in the French forests. Each line of one of Corot's misty landscapes, like every melody in a Chopin nocturne, seems somehow broader than a line ought to be. And this breadth is the result of the myriad glints of light and color that play along that line and, eventually, become essential to its definition.

But in Corot's paintings there is something behind all the mistiness that gives shape and strength, the legacy perhaps of his early years of study in Italy. In Chopin, too, there is more than merely an undirected flow of prettiness and sentimentality. He was conscious of the importance of an overall shape in a composition of any size, and his finest piano pieces are as controlled and disciplined in their flow as a Haydn symphony. Like Schumann, he had the power to deal with his personal expression with logic and shapeliness.

England's great romantic painter was John Constable, who brought to landscapes an atmosphere much the same as Corot's. Along with his contem-

The Book of Ossian, a synthetic but convincing re-creation of ancient, bardic legend, inspired romantic composers from Beethoven to Mahler, and its mood is also captured in Ingres's *Dream of Ossian* (opposite). Above: The violinist-composer Paganini, painted by Delacroix.

206

porary, William Turner, Constable instituted a short-lived English "school" of painters who moved away from the French painters' classical regard for proportion, and who made striking use of color and diffused line to instill their canvases with a point of view that was largely romantic.

However, England did not take as wholeheartedly to the romantic outpouring as did France and central Europe. Under the watchful and prudish eye of the Victorians a sentimental, story-telling style, brightly colored and genteel, dominated painting. Victorian architecture was, to some extent, a return to the classic inspirations of a century before, but it was crusted with a heavy Gothic overlay of nonfunctional ornamentation. The Pre-Raphaelite Brotherhood sought to return all art to the fifteenth-century outlook. It worked with an intricate vocabulary of archaic symbolism, took inspiration from legend and pageantry, and peopled its scenes with impeccable, ascetic gentlemen and ladies devoid of the sensuousness of continental romanticism.

The composer most prized by Victorian tastes was not the sensuous Chopin, but the cool and rational Felix Mendelssohn, whose orientation in the romantic world was the most classic. Mendelssohn shared many of the romantic ideas, and such works as his *Fingal's Cave* Overture and the *Scottish* Symphony use the orchestra brilliantly to paint murky seascapes. But it was a refined, restrained mode of expression, set quite clearly into classic frames. And, specifically for his English audiences, Mendelssohn attempted something of a latter-day Handelian style in his oratorios *Elijah* and *Saint Paul*, works as elegantly Pre-Raphaelite in their ascetic chastity as the most extravagant canvas by Sir Edward Burne-Jones.

However, Mendelssohn, who had won early glory in Germany by sparking a revival of the music of Bach, was not the only romantic composer to nurture the ideals of the musical past. The same must be said for the last of the romantic symphonists, Johannes Brahms. An enthusiastic disciple and protégé of Schumann in his early years, Brahms took a somewhat different course from the exuberant romantics as his style developed. He was deeply impressed with his studies of Bach, and worked into his own orchestral textures an intricate

208

*C*omposer Charles Gounod, whose own operas—among them *Faust* and *Romeo and Juliet*—expressed romantics' love for strong and tragic drama, is memorably sketched by Ingres.

harmonic style and a kind of irregular, dynamic, spiraling melodic language that was in many ways an outgrowth of the German baroque manner.

Brahms was little interested in the flamboyant virtuosity of the times. In his concertos, as in those of Mozart and Beethoven, the solo instrument and the orchestra are on an equal footing, with a sense of intimate conversation rather than personal heroism. His symphonies, lengthy and scored for a large orchestra rather thickly used, are completely abstract and their materials are organized in an almost classic manner.

Yet Brahms was not entirely divorced from romantic influences. His songs and short piano pieces are, like those of Schumann and Chopin, evocative mood studies. He could, when required, create as soaring and immediate a melody as any of his colleagues. But the cragginess of his large-scale scores, their intense crowding of detail, and their adherence to principles commonly observed a century before his time, make Brahms a latter-day synthesis of classicism and baroque romanticism.

209

REALISM AND NATIONALISM

The personalization of art was not the entire story of the romantic movement. An era of strong feelings naturally spawned elements of strong counterfeeling. Intense, personal emotion was opposed, on the one hand, by a new resurgence of naturalism and, on the other, by the phenomenon of nationalism—public, mass, and therefore nonpersonal.

Both movements joined in a searching-out of artistic models allied with the common man. We have seen that around 1800 there was a surge of interest in folk poetry and legend. Some of it was turned into high art in the lyrics of Goethe, and Schubert in turn captured these lyrics in music. The Germans, in particular, continued to be fascinated by folk art, especially the sense of the fantastic in the mythology of ancient Nordic tribes.

Carl Maria von Weber captured this in his opera *Der Freischütz*—an outgrowth of the *singspiel* in that it dealt with ordinary people and used spoken dialogue instead of the stylized recitative of the Italian opera. *Der Freischütz*, whose setting is a small German village, tells the story of a hero who sells his soul to a demon in return for magic bullets. Woven throughout the story are simple songs and dances which, for all their rusticity, are of high artistic level.

*H*onoré Daumier's wit, compassion, and sardonic cruelty were turned to subjects of the past, like Don Quixote and Sancho Panza (opposite) and also to contemporary scenes, like these house musicians during performance of a tragedy (below).

211

Furthermore, the scene of the casting of the bullets at midnight in the mysterious Wolf's Glen has a wide range of orchestral effects that greatly expands the dramatic vocabulary of the operatic orchestra.

Weber's opera gave birth to a host of descendants, all of which sought in some way to deal with the realities of rustic life with realistic rustic music. Some were serious in tone (as was *Der Freischütz*), but more were comic. The late manifestations were the brilliant, light comic operas of Johann Strauss II in which a rather more urbane group of characters than was usual in opera sang and acted to the constant strains of the waltz.

This kind of realism, with its strong folkloristic overtones, took root in other countries as well. The French painter Gustave Courbet brought rural scenes onto his canvases with naturalism and compassion. Honoré Daumier created biting satires out of life's seediness. Jean François Millet caught scenes of farm life with deeply compassionate emotion. Millet's *The Angelus* hung in practically every Victorian parlor, and inspired an equally well-known poem, *The Man With the Hoe*, by the American Edwin Markham.

The desire of composers to portray their native lands in music is understandable against the background of European history in the nineteenth century. It was a time of revolution and of the emergence of small nations across the continent. Italy's patriotic fervor permeated the operas of Giuseppe Verdi, as France's had guided the pen of Berlioz. To the east, Mikhail Glinka brought Russian folk accents into his operas and songs, even though the former were modeled largely after the Italian works of his time. In Bohemia, Antonin Dvorak and Bedrich Smetana paraphrased the folk songs and dance rhythms of their land in their large-scale orchestral and vocal works, and, to the north, Edvard Grieg accomplished much the same for Norway.

Neither Weber, Verdi, Glinka, Dvorak, Smetana, nor Grieg merely copied out his native music, however. They were true creators who steeped themselves in their native background until the spirit of their country's music infused their own style. Thus they could create new and original music that was subtly and inextricably related to a national language. Dvorak, in particu-

212

*S*ome romantic artists, among them the composer Brahms and the sculptor Carpeaux, clung to past principles. Carpeaux's *Ugolino and His Sons* (below) retains a neoclassic flavor. Not so Millet's *Potato Planters,* another naturalistic study of the life of common folk.

lar, operated with considerable success in the more "international" romantic style, creating a symphonic and chamber music language much like that of Brahms. But the particular nature of the Bohemian folk song, with its irregular accents and its powerful, surging emotionality, gave his music a special flavor. And Smetana created in his folk opera *The Bartered Bride* a richly humorous picture of rural life that manages to endear itself to audiences everywhere.

Other composers, as well, essayed the nationalistic style. Although he was to become the darling of the international musical scene, Franz Liszt recalled his origins in his Hungarian Rhapsodies for piano, brilliant technical exercises which used the exotic scales and languorous minor-mode harmonies of gypsy music for their principal material. And Brahms, though not Hungarian himself, caught the same spirit in his brief but skillful Hungarian Dances.

215

ROMANTIC OPERA

One of the paradoxes of musical romanticism is that, while it sought to deal with highly emotional states of mind and the larger-than-life expression of thoughts and images, it did so ideally through the medium of instrumental music. Perhaps, from one standpoint, it is not so great a paradox. After all, it was also in the nature of romanticism to cultivate an imprecise art, to blur outlines and leave meanings somewhat indistinct. That could not be so easily accomplished with words.

At any rate, Schubert, Schumann, Chopin, Mendelssohn, Liszt, and Brahms left behind no operas of any consequence. The operatic world was dominated for at least the first half of the century by the Italians and, to a lesser extent, by the French. German opera, which could trace its real beginnings to Weber's *Der Freischütz*, remained comparatively in shadow until the emergence around 1850 of Richard Wagner.

At the beginning of the nineteenth century Italian opera was thought out along two lines. First there was the simple, clear, and charming comic opera, which Cimarosa had derived from Pergolesi, and whose finest exponent was Mozart, an Austrian. Then there was the more old-fashioned lyric opera, descended from the Neapolitan school of the late baroque, somewhat less extravagant now, but still dependent upon the expression of lofty but not very profound sentiments in an extremely artificial plot-setting, with music intended mostly to show off the beauty of the human voice.

*L*ater to become one of the prime movers toward new horizons, Manet showed in his earlier paintings, like *The Guitarist,* an adherence to earlier ideals.

In France, the dominant form was the large-scale, lavish opera typified by the "horror-and-rescue" scores of Cherubini. These were on an even more lavish scale than the Italian serious operas and were full of extravagant, unsubtle heroic and patriotic gestures. Elaborate scenic designs, beloved by the French since the time of Lully, were demanded, and the stage was filled out with huge choruses and quite often by long dance sequences which provided further decoration at the expense of dramatic continuity. France also kept a comic opera tradition of much smaller scope, elegant and refined, full of reasoned charm and tenderness.

Basically, these styles held sway until well into the nineteenth century, due to the fact that there were superior practitioners involved. Gioacchino Rossini, Gaetano Donizetti, and Vincenzo Bellini raised the level of both comic and serious Italian opera immeasurably through their brilliant harmonic skill and their willingness to pit increased orchestral activity against the egos of their singers. Rossini, in particular, developed a charming patter-style in which the principal melodic material was carried by the orchestra against much more fragmentary vocal lines. This, coupled with his special "trademark," a mighty crescendo built up out of short, repeated phrases, gave his best comedies a breadth and flexibility unknown before. Rossini also worked in a grandiose, dramatic manner strongly influenced by the French style, and his *William Tell*, written for Paris, had a depth and range of orchestral color that aroused the admiration of Berlioz.

Donizetti gave heightened dramatic potential to opera by combining the best from both the serious and the comic Italian styles into a more rational, less artificial manner. He was also more careful than his predecessors in choosing good, workable plots and texts for his operas, and he rose to their requirements with a style that depended for most of its effect on long-arched melodies of sentimental immediacy. Like Rossini, he kept the orchestra busy; in the crucial wedding scene of *Lucia di Lammermoor*, the orchestra carries practically the entire melodic burden until the climatic Sextet.

Bellini was, by these standards, a more conservative composer. His operas' plots tended to be static and artificial, and his musical instinct seemed more an outgrowth of the Neapolitan school than of contemporary trends. But Bellini's musical tendencies were not completely old-fashioned. His gift for creating a slow, lyric melody line, capable of great poignancy when controlled by an intelligent singer, places him closer to the romantic tradition than either Donizetti or Rossini. Bellini's bel canto style, in which the line rested on a simple foundation of harmonic figuration, was greatly admired by Chopin, and its effect on some of Chopin's more sentimental compositions is unmistakable.

It was Giuseppe Verdi, however, who established romantic Italian opera

217

as a stronger, more individualistic dramatic entity than it had been at any time since its beginnings. A follower of Donizetti and Bellini early in his career, Verdi developed an individual style only slowly, as his sense of dramatic values heightened. Probably no operatic composer was ever so much in love with the theater as was Verdi, and it showed in his work. He set plays of Shakespeare, Schiller, and many minor Spanish and Italian playwrights to compelling musical translations, because he knew the essence of the stage almost as well as the authors themselves.

In the Verdi operas the final vestiges of the old formalism crumbled. He gradually broke down the long-standing distinction between recitative and aria in favor of a musical line that was more flexible and more consistently attuned to the pace of the drama. He trampled on the tradition of the singers' domination, dealing ruthlessly with virtuosos who attempted to insert added ornamentation and cadenzas to his own soaring melodic lines.

Verdi also returned to Italian opera the art of ensemble writing. No better understanding of his skill with the operatic ensemble can be gained than by comparing the famous Quartet in the last act of his *Rigoletto* with the equally famous Sextet in Donizetti's *Lucia di Lammermoor*. Both ensembles deal with conflicting emotions among the participating personalities, but, while Donizetti combines his voices for the most part in mellifluous, note-against-note harmony, Verdi sets each role apart from its fellows by its own sharply distinct melodic line. As Mozart had in the eighteenth century, Verdi made nineteenth-century Italian opera a drama of conflicts expressed through counterpoint.

His operas range from the most tender, sentimental tragedies (*La Traviata*), through the most absurd, robust, complicated dramas of passion and deception (*Il Trovatore*), to lavish works of epic grandeur (*Don Carlo*, *Aida*). In the final flowering of his style he created two Shakespearian masterpieces of vastly different mood, both of which stand as the most sublime musical translations of the Stratford master ever achieved. In *Otello* he fills out the violently emotional story with music that seems to entwine with every slight dramatic urging. And in *Falstaff* he underscores the laughter of the *Merry Wives of*

*A*merican Thomas Cole's 1836 painting, *The Consummation of Empire,* is vast jumble of history, allegory, pomp, and display—an apt counterpart of such grandiose pageant-operas as Meyerbeer's *The Huguenots* and Rossini's *Semiramide.*

219

Windsor with a nimble, racing counterpoint. It is the climax, as well as the twilight, of the Italian comic art.

The course of French opera was not so studded with geniuses, although the forms remained valid and popular. The successor to Cherubini was the German immigrant Giacomo Meyerbeer, whose vast historical pageants (*Les Huguenots, L'Africaine*) made up in massive scenic effects what they lacked in music. Meyerbeer was a clever composer rather than a skillful one. He had a rudimentary sense of melody and some interesting ideas on tone color, but his operas were produced more for entertainment than uplift. Berlioz himself essayed the Meyerbeer style with considerably more interesting results in his six-hour panorama, *Les Troyens*, based on the story of Aeneas.

After Meyerbeer, the French seemed to lose interest in this kind of opera, although Verdi produced for Paris a few examples in this grandiose style and prospered through them. On the whole, however, a somewhat gentler, more sentimental style took over. It was formalized and without much pretense to realism, but the men who attempted it (Charles Gounod, Ambroise Thomas, Georges Bizet) were well received. Bizet, however, became an important composer only when he threw off this artificial manner and created, in *Carmen*, a work as ornamental in its emotions as one of Goya's bloodstained studies of the horrors of war or poverty.

The climax of the French comic manner came in the works of another German émigré, Jacques Offenbach, who brought to his works a high quotient of biting, satiric wit. In Offenbach's best works he and his authors lampoon brilliantly the elegant French manners of the time, often paraphrasing them as allegories distantly based on characters in Greek mythology and legend. For example, in his *Orpheus in Hades* the musician who had been so poignantly transfigured by Monteverdi and Gluck becomes a vain and pompous café violinist, while his beloved Eurydice becomes a shrew whose death is generally welcomed. Offenbach worked into his comedies the popular French dances of the day, most spectacularly the lively and suggestive can-can. He also attempted, once only, the more serious and sentimental French style, producing

220

the uneven but powerful *Tales of Hoffmann.*

The young Richard Wagner was attracted by the French style, and his first major opera, *Rienzi,* was clearly influenced by the grandiose Meyerbeer manner. But the strength of his own convictions, along with his deep concern for the integrity of German art, soon led him along other paths. His *Flying Dutchman* and *Lohengrin,* the first inspired by an old Teutonic legend and the second by medieval Flemish history blended with mysticism, are both deeply in the debt of Weber, with his brilliant use of the orchestra to create supernatural effects and his development of a sturdy Germanic style colored by the sharp outlines and rich harmonic implications of folk music.

Then Wagner went into a short period of semiretirement which he gave over to a deep, introspective speculation on the nature of music and drama. If he had produced nothing for the stage beyond the three dramas already mentioned, plus the less successful but similar *Tannhäuser,* he would still be remembered as a most skillful creator of German opera in the Weber tradition.

He is, however, remembered for a great deal more than that. The mature Wagnerian style was not an abrupt break with his musical antecedents; it car-

*W*agner's quest for an epic retelling of ancient legend is mirrored in this etching, *The Finding of Arthur,* from Gustave Doré's Arthurian series. Above: Piano-design by 1830 had reached same complexity of décor as that of harpsichords 150 years earlier.

223

ried existing ideas to a higher development than even their originators had. Wagner's mature developments in the writing of music-drama had to do with creating an art form that would be the perfect union of words, music, and the visual arts. All must flow, with the avoidance at all costs of any intrusive element or note of artifice.

Thus, for example, there came about the complete integration between the singer and the orchestra, each equally concerned with the presentation of the drama at hand. There were no finite and formal arias; instead the singer was given a line of music merged completely with word-rhythms, free and without artificial demarcation. The orchestra became a dominant force in the drama, playing a contrapuntal web of melodic fragments immediately identifiable with the personages or concepts. Often, therefore, the orchestra served as a commentator or intermediary between the singer and the audience.

In order to maintain this sense of flow, Wagner loosened the already flexible harmonic practice of his era to the point where there is a purposeful suspension, for long periods at a time, of any real sense of harmonic direction. His concept of "endless melody" really meant "endless harmony," whereby the whole classic idea of coming to distinct and frequent tonal punctuation was abandoned. In Wagner's mature scores, one seldom arrives at any real recognition of a tonality until the end of an act.

Was this an innovation? Not entirely. Haydn's *Creation* begins with an orchestral passage representing Chaos in which cadences are constantly avoided to enhance the atmosphere. The finale of Beethoven's Ninth Symphony evolves a melody only after a blurred and chaotic beginning; the first movement of the same symphony also begins in a harmonic fog that defines no key for nearly half a minute. Schumann often left the endings of his songs and piano pieces unfinished-sounding.

With Wagner, however, these special effects become integrated into a consistent musical language. Very often, too, his dramatic thinking takes the form of an almost symphonic plan. Just as the opening motive of Beethoven's *Eroica* is rounded out to a full theme only at the end of the first movement,

Contemporary metaphysical stagings of Wagner's Ring music-dramas may well take their cue from Alfred Ryder's cloudy depiction of Siegfried and the Rhine Maidens.

225

so does the love music in the second act of *Tristan und Isolde* reach its full shaping only when repeated and expanded in Isolde's "Liebestod" at the end of the third act.

*N*euschwanstein, fantastic castle designed and built by Wagner's patron, Emperor Ludwig II of Bavaria.

Wagner did not work these naturalistic devices within a naturalistic framework, however. His mature dramas are concerned with the workings of supernatural forces and are set in murky, distant times. *The Ring of the Nibelungen*, comprising four operas, tells in a huge and convoluted allegory the life and death of idealized mankind. *Parsifal* is a mystical meditation on faith; *Tristan und Isolde*, the distillation of love frustrated and love triumphant. Only in *Die Meistersinger von Nürnberg* does he deal with the elements of the human comedy, and there it is partially to tell his personal story of the free artist triumphant over petty criticism.

Wagner is, then, in the mainstream of romanticism, with Liszt and Berlioz in the grandeur of his passions and the extravagance of his designs. Like them, he evolved musical forms that had some vestiges of past models, but which were violently expressive of a new spirit. The largeness of design, the blurring of outlines within that design, the intense bearing-down on a single mood, and that mood one of deep emotion—all these define Wagner as perhaps the archetypical romantic.

One fact is vitally significant. At the same time that Wagner, in *Tristan*, *Parsifal*, and the *Ring*, had evolved a harmonic language in which the sense of tonality was blurred, in which the push toward a clearly defined key was no longer the primary musical aim, Edouard Manet was producing the first paintings that embodied his belief in the blurring of colors, and in which the clear definition of the horizon was no longer the primary pictorial aim.

Early in the fifteenth century, the painters and composers at the Burgundian court, working in proximity with each other, had evolved tonality and the horizon as the overriding points of reference in their respective arts. The concepts were born together, endured together for four centuries. Now, just past the midway mark in the nineteenth century, they suddenly began to disappear together.

11. Since Wagner

The Tonal Heritage

*T*he Wagnerian revolution—no weaker word will suffice—provided musical thought with a crisis such as it had not faced since the time of the camerata at the beginning of the seventeenth century. In fact, it is possible to say that its effect was the establishment of two major pathways in the history of musical composition since about 1870: that leading directly from Wagner, and that which has attempted, not always with total success, to overlook or skirt the implications of Wagnerism.

Wagner's mature style had demonstrated that music could communicate powerful emotions, and that it could exist without the strict tonality which had hitherto been taken as inevitable. Thus the whole system on which the large musical forms, both operatic and symphonic, had depended for logic and order was suddenly questioned, if not openly challenged. True, the challenge to tonality had precedents as far back as that dark, indeterminate opening of Beethoven's Ninth Symphony, but never before had it been so forcefully presented. Just as the creators of the baroque style had blared "down with counterpoint," so did Wagner and his disciples, at least by implication, question the need for tonality in its classic sense.

There is an inconsistency, though, in this analogy. Within a few decades the baroque *stile rappresentativo* had swept through most of Europe. Following Wagner, on the other hand, there remained—and still remains—a large group of composers whose work was relatively uninfluenced by his ideas. Two streams of thought coexisted throughout the musical world in the last decades of the nineteenth century, occasionally absorbing ideas from one another, yet maintaining a high degree of individuality.

Musical nationalism, for example, remained relatively untouched by the Wagnerian influence. Men like Dvorak, Smetana, and Grieg had set their works in clear musical forms that stemmed directly from those of the earlier traditionalists, Schumann and Brahms in particular. And at the same time that Wagner's *Tristan* burst on the scene, Russia was making its entrance into the musical world. So rich was her heritage of native music that Russia's composers saw no need to cultivate the Wagnerian style.

230

The first important Russian composer was Mikhail Glinka, whose early years had been spent absorbing the operatic styles of Meyerbeer and the Italian romantics. He returned to his native land with a fervent desire to infuse these ideals with Russian spirit, and succeeded at least once—in his masterpiece, *A Life for the Czar*. It is a curious work, which leaps easily and constantly from the lavish melodic manner of Bellini to the oriental scales and irregular phrase structures of Russian folksong. It is Russian, too, in its emphasis on choral effects and other massive devices.

The next generation of Russian composers, however, brought the country's musical ambitions to full and explosive fruition. A group including Alexander Borodin and Modest Mussorgsky banded together for this very purpose. The "Five," as they called themselves, were for the most part musical amateurs, but they addressed themselves with professional zeal to creating a national music infused with the sounds and spirit of folksong.

The most remarkable product of Russia's new-found musical expression was Mussorgsky's *Boris Godunov*, an opera based on Pushkin's drama about the conniving sixteenth-century czar. In the original version of this work (well-meaning friends later got the composer to add such "western" elements as a love scene) we find an opera almost totally free of either Italian or German influence. Vocal lines follow irregular, rhapsodic patterns closely allied to the rhythms of Russian speech; the orchestra is full of purposeful crudities and clashes of timbre that compellingly underline the barbarity of the story. Opportunities for hearing this score as Mussorgsky envisioned it are extremely rare. It is most often heard in a version much smoothed out by a far less visionary member of the Five, Nikolai Rimsky-Korsakov.

The time of the Five was also the time of a resurgence of painting in Russia, although no artist of lasting significance emerged. Vassily Surikov and Ilya Repin, painted realistic subjects in vibrant colors that are akin to the orchestral colors of Borodin and Mussorgsky. Indeed, one minor architect-painter, Viktor Hartmann, lives on because Mussorgsky composed a set of short tone pictures for piano, *Pictures at an Exhibition*, interpreting musically

*O*pening pages: In paintings like Monet's *Waterloo Bridge*, traditional artistic attitudes toward clean lines and pictorial exactitude were replaced by a blurred, impressionistic style. Similarly, in Wagner's music, clear-cut harmonic basis of music that had prevailed for centuries began to disintegrate.

a series of Hartmann's paintings of Russian life. Here, nationalist artist and nationalist composer made common cause.

Russia's other great composer of the late nineteenth century, Peter Ilich Tchaikovsky, was not actually a member of the Five, although many of his works show a kindred spirit. Actually, Tchaikovsky's musical interests were far broader than those of his countrymen, and his musical training was considerably more solid. While he could turn out symphonic poems and other descriptive pieces in which Russian folk songs were interwoven, he could also produce pieces of more abstract design, Russian perhaps in their intense emotionality, but organized along lines of the Germanic symphonic repertory.

232

Other countries, as well, witnessed stirrings of artistic consciousness in the late decades of the century, countries whose culture in former times had been largely imported. In Poland, Stanislaw Moniuszko produced a number of nationalistic operas, of which *Halka* is still occasionally revived. In Hungary there was Ferenc Erkel, also primarily an operatic composer. And to the north, in Finland, Jan Sibelius reawakened his country's national consciousness with a large repertory of vocal and orchestral music, in which he translated the sights and moods of his native countryside into tonal terms, though only occasionally employing actual folk music. Sibelius, whose career ran well into the twentieth century, was strongly under Tchaikovsky's influence when he began his work. The individuality of his mature style lies in his strikingly bleak orchestration and the tension he creates by playing melodic material first in a fragmentary state and only later fusing it into longer tunes.

As the new century began, a pattern of cultural emergence was, in fact, making itself clear. Countries previously overshadowed began to assert their artistic individuality. Much of this spirit was the consequence of political change, of revolutions large and small that created new nations or at least furthered aspirations toward nationality.

Nationalistic expression, in music as in all arts, is by nature conservative. That is, it uses material that has long been in existence—folk songs, folk images, folk lore—and deals with it in ways sufficiently simple to preserve its basic outline. The nationalistically-oriented artist attempts to communicate to a large audience his enthusiasm for his own particular heritage, and tends to do so in terms that are uncomplex and direct.

The term conservative, which will occur frequently in connection with artistic trends in our own century, implies no value judgment. Bach was a conservative, in the sense that he worked with styles and modes of expression that had been well-established before his time; so was Handel, and for similar reasons. To the extent an artist has the imagination to use familiar and accepted elements in original ways, he might be called a radical conservative. Such are Bach, Handel, and Mussorgsky, and they stand at some remove from

*I*n Russia and other countries on the fringes of artistic mainstreams, a new awareness of traditions and native heritage was expressed in art: in operas using folk-musical styles, and in paintings—like Repin's *Cossacks Writing A Letter to the Czar*—dealing with native subjects.

233

the less original conservatives such as Grieg and Rimsky-Korsakov.

The broad outlines of nineteenth-century musical organization were retained by the musical conservatives. They continued writing symphonies, concertos, large-scale operas in the Verdi-Meyerbeer tradition, chamber works, songs, and piano pieces of smaller dimension. The orchestra they used was the large, massive ensemble developed by Brahms and Liszt. Nationalistic-minded composers often used it to create effects peculiar to a region and a people, as in the music of Sibelius and the Russians.

Late in the nineteenth century a group of English composers began to repair their country's serious lack of a native musical repertory. In its first generation, Sir Edward Elgar worked with a style largely shaped by his early studies on the continent. It was a style quite close to that of Brahms, but broader and more leisurely, with an energy and robustiousness that reflected England's persisting fondness for the massive Handelian sound.

The individuality of the English style was more fully shaped, however, in the ensuing generations. Ralph Vaughan Williams worked into his large-scale scores not only the lilt of the English folksong, but also the distinctive elegance and harmonic resource of such Renaissance composers as Thomas Morley and William Byrd. For example, his Fifth Symphony, composed in the 1940's, achieves much of its effect from the use of modal scales. So does his most popular work, the *Fantasia on a Theme by Tallis,* in which the string orchestra uses echo effects to suggest the atmosphere of an ancient cathedral.

*T*homas Eakins' *The Pathetic Song* illustrates appeal at his time—the late 18th century—of subjects that told simple stories in direct, simple manner. It suggests, too, salon style popular in music of same period.

Vaughan Williams' establishment of a symphonic style that can be thought of as indigenous has been bolstered by later composers like William Walton and Benjamin Britten. Walton's major work has been in symphonic forms, and such works as his Second Symphony and Violin Concerto clearly suggest a direct line of descent, through Elgar, from the German romantics. Britten, though he has written a number of fluent and well-made orchestral scores, is primarily known as a composer for the voice. His grand opera, *Peter Grimes,* contains much that could be considered a tribute to *Boris Godunov,* notably its massed choral passages.

234

The growth of the conservative style in the United States closely parallels that in England. Naturally, there was no previous American tradition of any importance to provide composers with inspiration, but there was a wealth of folksong and folk art extending back to the times of the first settlers, and this in time proved fertile ground. The first important American generation was largely a product of European training; the works of men like Edward MacDowell and John Knowles Paine around the turn of the century are important for little more than the historical fact of their existence.

By 1920, however, something more indigenous began to make itself felt in American music. Most composers still acquired their basic training in Europe's conservatories, but they returned to their native land determined to

236

make use of the materials it offered them. Sometimes this determination was expressed with unfortunate naïveté, as in the case of George Gershwin. A composer of definite gifts in the popular field, Gershwin attempted to use these gifts in a symphonic style, creating his rhapsodies and concertos, and folk opera *Porgy and Bess*. His aim was to combine the popular idiom with Lisztian or Mussorgskian models, and while the materials are undeniably attractive, the works themselves are seriously flawed as artistic entities.

Nevertheless, composers persisted in working with the elements of Americana on a large scale, and some efforts were successful. Roy Harris and, even more notably, Aaron Copland, have successfully introduced jazz and folk elements into symphonies and other major works. Copland's ballet scores

237

make use of cowboy tunes and early American hymns. His style in these scores is not very much more dissonant than that of Tchaikovsky, but Copland creates a peculiar pungency through his use of bright, brassy orchestral effects. Another American of decidedly conservative leanings, Virgil Thomson, has developed a fascinating individual style from delving into old hymn books.

The most individualistic of the indigenous American composers, however, were two men whose style was entirely home-grown—the New Englanders Charles Ives and Carl Ruggles. Ives, born in 1874, was an unruly and exciting experimenter. Working almost entirely with material derived from popular American hymns and ballads, combined with a few original tunes of no great distinction, Ives evolved a style of fearsome complexity. By working two or three ideas against each other contrapuntally, but with no apparent regard for

238

What Grant Wood did for American farm scene, Reginald Marsh did for urban life; opposite, his *Wooden Horses*. In Mexico, Orozco worked with brush dipped in social consciousness to create patterns out of humble life of Mexican lower classes, as in *Zapatistas*.

the classic rules of counterpoint, he created dissonances so grating that few took his music seriously during his lifetime. It is being unearthed now, its power somewhat easier for today's more attuned audiences to approach. Ruggles, too, worked in an individualistic dissonant style, jamming massive, granitic blocks of sound against each other.

The rise of an indigenous American music from earlier, European-inspired models was paralleled by the emergence of a distinctive native style in painting. There had been American primitive painters, sculptors, and craftsmen since colonial days, of course. But late in the nineteenth century the painters of importance were men like Winslow Homer and Thomas Eakins, whose styles were influenced by French contemporaries. The decades after the First World War saw a new generation of American painters, who sought in

239

an artfully homespun way to capture the life around them and give it an unmistakable native flavor, as composers were attempting to do in their music. Thomas Hart Benton and Grant Wood succeeded in creating a distinctive American rural style, and Reginald Marsh did the same for city life.

Similar trends can be observed in Latin America, particularly in the roughhewn work of the Mexican composer, Carlos Chavez, and his painter-colleagues Diego Rivera and José Orozco, who worked with the primitive sights and sounds of Mexican peasant life. The Brazilian composer, Heitor Villa-Lobos, also caught the rhythms of his native land in his huge output of tone poems.

The dawn of the twentieth century saw a rekindling of musical activity in Spain. Enrique Granados, the first major Spanish composer of modern times, devoted most of his brief lifetime to capturing in songs and piano works the same Spanish spirit that had been immortalized a century before in the paintings of Goya. His successor, Manuel de Falla, carried the work further in a small but brilliant repertory that included orchestral works, vocal pieces, and short operas dealing with Spanish life.

Meanwhile, the nationalistic trends that had begun in eastern Europe far back in the nineteenth century continued to shape the music of that region. The great successor to Dvorak and Smetana in the area now known as Czechoslovakia was Leos Janacek. Unlike his predecessors, Janacek came from the province of Moravia, and his folk heritage was colored by a deep exoticism, even at times an orientalism, that is missing in the more Germanic folk music of Bohemia. With great mastery he worked this heritage into a repertory of orchestral and choral music and, in a series of operas, he combined it with a deep love of nature.

Russian nationalism was carried forward for a time in the works of Igor Stravinsky, a disciple of Rimsky-Korsakov, whose earliest orchestral works and songs had stamped him as a worthy successor to the Five. But Stravinsky was soon to strike out on new paths. True, throughout his career he has produced scores with elements directly stemming from his Russian origins, but

240

his later scores, after his break with Russia, do not aim at purely nationalistic expression.

More truly nationalistic was the music of Serge Prokofiev and Dimitri Shostakovich. Prokofiev, who lived much of his life outside Russia, wrote in a variety of styles stemming from such influences as the virtuosic Liszt tradition and the latter-day shadow of the German symphonic form. Yet his most popular scores are unmistakably Russian: the cantata *Alexander Nevsky* (derived from a film score) and the satiric opera *Love for Three Oranges*. Shostakovich, an avowed and avid nationalist, has composed works in continuing loyalty to his native Russian heritage, and in conformity with official attitudes toward that heritage. His style is brilliant and somewhat superficial, with an orchestral palette clearly derived from the Five and from Tchaikovsky.

Possibly the most systematic approach to the development of a nationalistic style was undertaken around the turn of the century in Hungary by that country's two most important composers, Zoltan Kodaly and Bela Bartok. Both men spent several years of their early careers among the people, carefully recording and deciphering the huge variety of scales, melodic patterns, and rhythms characteristic of native Hungarians. (These are not to be confused with the gypsy elements in the "Hungarian" music of Brahms and Liszt.) These researches provided both composers with a rich musical language out of which their individual styles were formed.

Of the two, Kodaly remained the more conservative composer. Bartok, on the other hand, plunged deeply into the spirit of his findings and created some of the most powerful and original music of our time. In his works the pounding, jagged, irregular rhythms of native folk dance often become a frenzied study in pure energy. Through constant experimentation he enlarged the range of instrumental music with a vast range of new possibilities, for instance using pianos and strings as percussive instruments. His exploration, however, is controlled by a strong sense of formal unity, rivaling that of Beethoven. Bartok's musical output testifies that music inspired by a specific national heritage can take its place in the international repertory.

241

242

ITALY AND FRANCE: THE REAL AND THE UNREAL

Although Italy felt the impact of Richard Wagner, and even his presence (Wagner died in Venice in 1883), the place of musical dominance had remained Verdi's. His was the heritage with which composers had to reckon, as long as opera remained the principal medium in public favor. The Verdi years had brought to the opera house a sense of dramatic integrity and realism that had dispelled conclusively the artifice of the bel canto era.

Verdi's heirs were numerous. They had heard Wagner and were aware of the emotional power of his dissonances, but they appeared quite disinterested in following his dictates in other respects. They chose, instead, to carry the emotional violence of the later Verdi—particularly his *Otello*—to new heights. To accomplish this, they sought out plots dealing with people of their own time, whose deep sufferings and occasional joys would be even more immediate to their audiences. And they sought to match these plots with music that furthered Verdi's attempt to break down the older, formalized division between recitative and aria. They sought to achieve greater dramatic verity with a completely continuous musical line punctuated by the natural rhythms of speech.

The public demanded drama and was rewarded with drama of strong violence set to music that drove home dramatic points in no uncertain terms. The first of these *verismo* operas to achieve fame was Pietro Mascagni's *Cavalleria Rusticana*, produced in 1890—three years before Verdi's *Falstaff*. The terse brutality of plot and music swept over audiences like thunder. Mascagni never again enjoyed such success, and the palm soon passed to the most talented of Verdi's successors, Giacomo Puccini, a man of almost unfailing theatrical shrewdness and an unmistakable gift for creating a soaring, sentimental, and immediate Italianate lyricism. Puccini has had many imitators; works in his style are still being created, both in Italy and abroad. Among his most successful heirs is the Italian-American Gian Carlo Menotti, who shares Puccini's innate sense of the theater.

The situation in France was far more complex. From early in the nineteenth century, it had been obvious that a new cultural independence had begun

*L*ast of great French impressionists, Renoir turned his attention to scenes of people enjoying themselves, here in a *Ball at Bougival.* Far left: Study in bronze of ballet dancer by Degas. Love of the dance was French tradition since time of Louis XIV.

243

Cezanne's Forest at Fontainbleau, with its interplay of light and shade, might be setting for opening scene of *Pelléas et Mélisande*. Opposite: Like Debussy and Ravel, Matisse drew inspiration from oriental art, as in clean, Japanese-inspired *Joie de Vivre*.

to take shape in that country. The French painters, as already observed, were the most influential in the nineteenth century, beginning with David and Delacroix and continuing through Corot and his colleagues. French operatic tastes, leaning as they did toward the spectacular works of Meyerbeer and, somewhat later, the more genial sentimentality of Gounod, dictated the workings of composers even beyond that country's border; both Wagner and Verdi came under the influence of the French when they composed operas for production by the Paris houses.

French composers did submit to some degree, however, to outside influences. The shadow of Wagnerian chromaticism fell over the work of César Franck (actually of Belgian birth, but active in Paris for most of his life), and

244

that of his major pupils Vincent d'Indy and Ernest Chausson. These men composed in large symphonic forms, organizing them in a manner strongly influenced by Schumann and Liszt. As in the Liszt tone poems, unity was achieved through the use of thematic transformation. One might say of the entire Franckian circle, in fact, that it worked toward transplanting much of the spirit of romantic Germanic music into France. Indigenously French elements—the simple dance rhythms, descriptive elements, or folk songs—played a relatively minor role in this music, although d'Indy's popular *Symphony on a French Mountain Air* does represent one sally in a nationalistic direction.

Somewhat more traditionally French in its approach was a second group of composers who sought to keep alive the elegance, clarity, and high crafts-

manship of the country's past, while at the same time reaching out for the sentiment and emotionality of romanticism. To this group belonged the prolific and long-lived Camille Saint-Saëns, in whose music one encounters the classic facility of the eighteenth-century rococo masters, the tender sighs of Chopin, more than a touch of Offenbach's frivolity, and even, as in the Third Symphony, a sidelong glance at Wagner. Two operatic composers of some merit, Jules Massenet and Gustave Charpentier, produced a repertory of lush, sentimental works that also mirrored this kind of eclecticism. The later exponent of this style, Gabriel Fauré, was far more successful in maintaining individuality in his simple, quiet output.

Of all French composers of the last years of the nineteenth century and the first decades of the twentieth, Fauré and Claude Debussy best expressed France's artistic developments. Both had begun their careers as exponents of the more-or-less generalized European romantic outlook and their early works, which tend toward virtuosity and flamboyance, are definitely in the manner of Franz Liszt.

Both were strongly influenced, as time went on, by the same trends that appealed to painters and poets of their time, a leaning toward the suggestion of effect, rather than its clear delineation, and a love of color for its own sake. Among the painters, Manet's blurred outlines and distortion of perspective were further explored by his successors, Auguste Renoir, Edgar Degas, and, especially, Claude Monet. In his landscapes, his studies of water lilies, even his pictures of cathedrals, Monet was less concerned with outline than with the play of light over objects. He added a new dimension to the observer's function by suggesting impressions of a scene rather than the scene itself. The technique came to be called "impressionism" from the title "Impression: Sunrise" given by a critic to a Monet canvas, and the name has stuck.

Impressionism is one of those artistic terms that can be extended with equal justice to many kinds of expression. What Monet and others had done in painting, poets like Mallarmé, Verlaine, and Baudelaire also accomplished with words, forming images that were indistinct and hazy rather than concrete.

246

Similarly, Fauré and Debussy worked with an impressionistic musical language—using chords for color rather than structural support, wisps of melody rather than fully formed melodic arches, fleeting touches of instrumental color rather than carefully organized sonorities. Beyond this, the two composers differ. Fauré, for all his feeling for color, worked within a clearly classic form and created music of an abstract quality directly related to classic models. Debussy, tending more to the short, coloristic piano or orchestral fragment, was more the "pure" musical painter.

It should be borne in mind that the harmonic obscurity achieved by Debussy, and by Fauré to some degree, is not the same kind of blurring used by Wagner in such works as *Tristan und Isolde*. Unlike Wagner, the French composers continued to work with a strong sense of tonality, even though their methods for defining that tonality were considerably more sophisticated than those of, say, Schubert. They enriched rather than expanded the tonal horizons. Debussy actually held Wagner in great distrust, as he wrote many times in his musical essays. Even though he does use such Wagnerian devices as the leitmotive in his opera *Pelléas et Mélisande*, there are vast differences between the two composers.

Debussy's influences did not stem solely from the impressionists. He was also deeply stirred by the music of the Orient, which was heard in Paris in the 1800's through a series of international exhibitions. He was attracted particularly to the music of Indonesia, with its exotic, percussive effects and the dreamlike monotony of its repetitive short phrases.

The clear, sharp lines of oriental paintings made a profound impression on many artists of the time and this was partly responsible for a movement that grew up around 1900, in some ways as a reaction against the impressionistic haze. Painters, architects, and sculptors formed a new art, or *Art Nouveau*, a distinctive decorative style that broke completely with impressionism in favor of something strongly outlined yet supple. Debussy's music incorporates some of this feeling too; the sinuous curve of the solo flute in his *Prelude to the Afternoon of a Faun* suggests the designs of *Art Nouveau*.

*T*urning his back on impressionism, espousing instead a clean-cut style both sinuous and immensely childlike, Aubrey Beardsley was one of the key figures in *l'Art Nouveau*—direct, popular, witty. Opposite is Beardsley's fantasized sketch of composer Carl Maria von Weber; above, "Stomach Dancer."

247

*P*rimitive yet
fantastic canvases of
part-time painter
Rousseau reflect reaction
against impressionism
that gave rise in music
to "white" style
of the Six. Like Erik
Satie's satiric
piano pieces, Rousseau's
Football Players
seem to have acquired
weightlessness.

Debussy's late works, in fact, show a simple clarity of outline that is far removed from impressionism. In his last scores, a set of three sonatas for various instrumental combinations, there is a new classicism, employing all of the latter-day harmonic sophistication, yet simple and direct.

Actually, by 1910 impressionism had been largely abandoned. The preceding years had produced the anti-impressionist paintings of such men as Pierre Bonnard and the strange, visionary primitives of Henri Rousseau. Now many artists were approaching their subject matter with a tendency toward sharp demarcations and sharper emotions. They exhibited a childlike delight in the juxtaposition of bright colors and a passion for depicting objects with an almost absurd simplicity. Something of this symbolic realism is seen in certain early works of Matisse and Picasso.

Neoclassicism found its musical expression in the works of the supreme scoffer, Erik Satie, and in the group of young composers who, in the early 1920's, formed *Les Six* under the spiritual guidance of the fantastic poet-painter Jean Cocteau.

The Six took their inspiration from many sources. Darius Milhaud found his in American jazz and in the native rhythms and percussive sounds of Brazil, which he had visited as a young man. Francis Poulenc found it in the music of Rameau and Couperin, and in the popular tunes of the dance halls of Paris. Arthur Honegger combined a hard-edged cabaret style with elements of medieval mysticism. Not a member of the group, but allied with its spirit, Maurice Ravel was inspired by Spanish rhythm and color, and by jazz as well.

From this group came a rich and attractive style, simple, yet full of special complications. It was predominantly tonal music, more consciously so than even that of Debussy. Yet one of the earmarks of the style was the occasional use of two or more tonalities heard simultaneously, each clearly identifiable, and yet with strong dissonances resulting from the clash.

And the most spectacular genius of the time, the Russian émigré-turned-Parisian, Igor Stravinsky, found in neoclassicism a congenial format for his ideas. Stravinsky, as has been noted, began his career much under the spell of

248

Picasso's *Evocation (Burial of Casagemas)*, painted in 1901, has folklike images and air of Gothic secrecy. In its primevalism, it is allied to such works of Stravinsky as *The Rite of Spring* and *Les Noces.*

Russian nationalism. By 1912, however, he had already exhausted the possibilities in the language of the Five, and had in his ballet *Petrouchka* moved on toward a more individualistic manner. Already in *Petrouchka*, predating the Six by a decade, examples can be found of two tonalities in simultaneous clash.

Stravinsky's next work, *The Rite of Spring*, was also Russian in inspiration in that it was a ballet about Russian pagan rituals, but it was conceived in terms that bore little discernible resemblance to the ideals of his teachers. The orchestra was expanded, not only in size but also in technique; at times the entire ensemble becomes a gigantic percussion instrument. This device is similar to the techniques being used at the time by Bela Bartok. The rhythmic scheme is extremely fluid; in some passages the basic meter changes from measure to measure. Melody, and harmony as we know it, are subordinated by the chaotic onslaught of rhythm and sonority. The *Rite* is one of music's great single forward steps; like the first operas or Beethoven's *Eroica*, it was a huge challenge suddenly flung at existing musical institutions.

At this point, Stravinsky did one of his many about-faces, and worked for a time with small, clean instrumental ensembles and a neoclassic sense of organization. His Octet for Winds is a seeming tribute to Mozart, and his ballet *The Soldier's Tale* uses simplistic material of the type expounded by Satie and the Six. Another ballet, *The Wedding*, returns to Russian folksong for its inspiration, but expresses it in clear, hard scoring that involves voices and an ensemble of pianos and percussion.

None of these composers seriously questioned the validity of the tonal system as it had existed since the Renaissance. None of the painters who worked close to them seriously questioned the validity of the concrete object as the basis for painting. True, the approach of both composer and painter was often free, motivated by a burning need to experiment, to test the limits to which accepted ideals might be stretched. And out of these experiments came works of striking validity and originality which established one possible direction for the artistic expression of our own day. Clearly, however, it was not the only possible direction.

12. The

Wagnerian Shadow

Wagnerian implications were vast. They touched every composer of Wagner's time and of the generations that immediately succeeded him. Even Verdi, who many regarded as the antithesis of Wagner, was accused of falling under the Bayreuth master's spell in *Aida*, where he uses leitmotives to identify principal characters, and abandons the traditional aria format in favor of a more continuous musical line. Wagner's rich, chromatic harmonic style influenced many French composers, as has been seen, and even those nationalistic conservatives who most openly resisted his methods learned much from him about orchestral grandeur.

But the Wagnerian heritage is most directly observed within the confines of the German-Austrian artistic world, at least until the dissolution of that world under Nazism. Wagner himself believed in his creation of the *Heilige deutsche Kunst*, to quote the final words of Hans Sachs in *Die Meistersinger*, and it was to the Germanic mind that he spoke most directly.

Anton Bruckner, the pious Austrian organist, worshipped him from afar, and drew heavily on certain elements of the Wagnerian language for the creation of his nine symphonies. These works, clumsy and uneven though they may be, have an undeniable emotional power which derives almost entirely from the composer's ready assimilation of Wagner's dramatic grandiosity. Their clumsiness lies primarily in Bruckner's attempt to force this seamless language into classic symphonic form, to which it was not adaptable.

Richard Strauss also came under the Wagnerian spell early in his career, and developed a melodic style strongly in debt to the older composer. This style, consisting of a long, sinuous, passionate declamation, irregular in its phrase lengths and seemingly free of any direct allegiance to a given key, served Strauss well in a series of brilliant orchestral tone poems produced during the 1890's, and won him widespread acclaim as Wagner's true heir. Along with this original melodic gift came a remarkable understanding of orchestral color.

But Strauss was not the original musical thinker that Wagner had been. After his initial successes he tended toward the cultivation of easy effects. His harmonic style was basically tonal, more so by far than Wagner's, and its modernity came from patches of dissonance grafted onto the simple framework. He made the mistake of abandoning his early Lisztian flamboyance in favor of an affected, more soft-spoken, neo-Mozartian clarity. Shorn of its external glitter, his style began to reveal its basic shortsightedness.

Neither Bruckner nor Strauss—nor a host of minor figures around them, including Max Reger, Hans Pfitzner, and Franz Schreker—had the insight to assess Wagner's musical message. Gustav Mahler came somewhat closer.

Mahler's personal artistic vision resembled that of Wagner. He, too, worked on the most grandiose scale. His huge symphonic structures involved oversized orchestras, choruses both onstage and off, solo voices, and, most important, programmatic content that dealt with struggle, triumph, and defeat. His musical ancestors, besides Wagner, were Beethoven and Schubert. The latter, in particular, supplied inspiration for Mahler's warm lyricism.

What makes Mahler seem the immediate heir of Wagner, however, is the mastery he shows in creating surging, chromatic harmony that is restless, rhapsodic, and passionate. If Bruckner and Strauss are Wagnerites, their heritage is largely drawn from the early Wagner. Mahler, especially in his final symphonies and the song-cycle, *Das Lied von der Erde*, took as his point of departure the mature and revolutionary Wagner of *Tristan* and *Parsifal*. He succeeded in expressing symphonically the poignance, frustration, and sense of tragedy that Wagner had instilled into these works. Emotion guided his pen. The language is intense, so much so that the results are often larger than life—larger and also distorted. Much of his message is expressed in caricature, in a wry cynicism that twists the simplest material into ill-tempered burlesque.

In this approach Mahler is allied to trends among German painters of his time. French artistic ideals had made inroads among German painters around 1890, not so much the impressionism of Monet and Renoir, but the intense, tortured inspiration of Vincent Van Gogh.

The introspection and loneliness expressed in Van Gogh's later paintings seemed to strike a responsive chord in many Germans, most notably Lovis Corinth. A romantic realist in his younger years, and devoted also to the bril-

*O*pening pages: Van Gogh's intensely personal fantasies, his obsession with "innerness" of the scene— as in *Starry Night*— greatly influenced expressionist movement in Germany in early 20th century.

255

*M*unch's *The Cry* (right) and Nolde's *The Prophet* (opposite) illustrate expressionist painter's desire to implant almost excessive emotion into a figure, which thereby becomes more symbol than object.

liance and lustiness of early Flemish art, Corinth later worked out a combination of traditional narrative realism and the blurring used by the impressionists. The result was a series of paintings in which naturalistic line is distorted and reformed into something having the effect of an anguished outcry. It is a metamorphosis of the real into the symbolic, not unlike the distension of reality that occurs in the works of Mahler.

As a mode of artistic communication it came to be known as expressionism. It can be defined as the use of art to show and epitomize the artist's state of mind. If the impressionist's brush was guided by visible surfaces, by the play of light over an object, the expressionist is guided instead by his emotions in their full power. Once again is seen the classic antithesis of the outward and the inward, of relaxation and tension.

Many elements shaped the expressionistic outlook. Its distortion and grotesquery were to a large extent a latter-day manifestation of the German Gothic. It is significant that in 1911, the year of Mahler's death and the year in which the word "expressionism" was first used, a series of concerts held in southern Germany gave the works of such Gothic composers as Machaut their first modern hearing. In the works of many of the first generation of German expressionist painters—notably Emil Nolde and Ernst Kirchner—the influence of medieval German woodcuts and the fantastic shapes of Hieronymus Bosch are readily discernible.

The primitivism of Paul Gauguin was also noted and assimilated into the movement. The elements that set Gauguin apart from his impressionist countrymen—the slashing, vibrant colors, the distortion of figure and perspective, the oneness of Man and his environment—these were features that the expressionists recognized and welcomed.

In the main, however, it was the German temperament, and the uneasy state of German affairs around the turn of the century, that gave expressionism its emotional validity. It was a time of disillusion and decline. Not only a century but an era had ended, and the evidence was everywhere apparent. It was this that brought Mahler to his questioning of simple values, and it was this

257

that inspired in such expressionist painters as Edvard Munch, George Grosz, and Oskar Kokoschka, all of whom spent much of their lives in Germany, an obsession with death and decadence and overt human agony.

The most forceful statements of expressionistic aims came out of Munich in 1911, from a group of artists in many fields who banded together under the name *Der blaue Reiter* (The Blue Horseman). Its spiritual leaders were the Russian-born painter Wassily Kandinsky and the German Franz Marc, and among its well-wishers were the Frenchman Georges Braque and the Spaniard Pablo Picasso. Its ranks also included the composer Arnold Schoenberg.

These were men of diverse ideals. Kandinsky had already published a monograph, *Concerning the Spiritual in Art*, which was a manifesto on art's inner life. In this work he examined the elements of painting—color, line, shape, and design—and found each of them self-sufficient as expressive symbols. From this theory he evolved a style which completely forswore representation, dealing instead with abstractions to which spiritual meanings could be imputed. Marc, unlike Kandinsky, worked with recognizable objects upon which he imposed in a unique manner his own emotional viewpoint.

Within expressionism, then, at least two basic approaches can be discerned: that of which Kandinsky was a major proponent, involving the integrity of the abstract, and that symbolized by Marc, in which the object persisted as the basis of the work. The history of the movement to the present day is, in fact, made all the more fascinating by the interplay between these ideals.

An even more fascinating element of the *Blaue Reiter* group is the interplay among the arts. Kandinsky, in his monograph and in his paintings themselves, proclaimed that his kind of abstraction represented the approach of painting to music, which had been proclaimed by ancient philosophers as the highest of all the arts. Representational painting, on the other hand, was diluted by its resemblance to literature, a lower art than music. Kandinsky dabbled in composition. Schoenberg tried his hand at painting, mainly guided by Kandinsky's precepts. It was one of those movements, like the group assembled at the Burgundian court in the fifteenth century, in which the arts met in

258

close proximity and derived much strength from each other.

Interestingly enough, many of Kandinsky's ideas on the relation of music and the visual arts, and especially on the spirituality of individual elements of the artistic language, were mirrored in the works of a man far removed from actual contact with the group, the Russian mystical composer Alexander Scriabin. Basically a romantic whose piano works mirrored the Chopin-Liszt tradition, Scriabin came late in life to a series of experiments in combining sound and sight. His tone poem *Prometheus* was meant to be accompanied by shifting colors flashed onto a screen by a projector worked from a keyboard. Scriabin's theories on the unity of sight and sound, especially those concerning a special harmony which he devised and which he called a "mystic chord," seem analogous to those of Kandinsky, but with music, rather than painting, as a point of departure. Scriabin, however, lacked the vision and the musical intensity to bring his ideas into world acceptance. It was, rather, from among the *Blaue Reiter* group, principally Kandinsky and Schoenberg, that the path to the future was mapped.

Schoenberg, Viennese by birth, had begun his career with a number of instrumental and choral works which were decidedly under the spell of *Tristan* and of Mahler—music in which tonality was discernible but extremely fluid, and in which chromaticism was used to create an atmosphere of deep yearning and passion. But influenced by Kandinsky, Schoenberg began to evolve a far more complicated musical style. His Five Pieces for Orchestra, composed in 1909, is the musical counterpart of Kandinsky's nonrepresentational paintings and theories: They are studies in pure color, with no attempt at classic structure. One of them, in fact, is built entirely on a single chord, through which orchestral tone colors ooze and shift. At about the same time, his two most important pupils of composition, Anton von Webern and Alban Berg, also produced sets of orchestral pieces in which color was the sole binding force.

As with most artistic movements, expressionism gradually began to evolve its own rules by which to control the high emotionalism of its early stages. By 1920, with Europe beginning to recover slowly from a disastrous war, artists

260

in all fields had begun a definite movement toward a new formalism. The inner tensions and mystical visions of *Blaue Reiter* painters were tempered under the influence of a group of architects at the Bauhaus in Weimar, led by Walter Gropius. These men evolved a style that was basically clean-cut and geometric. Straight lines, slab-like rectangles, and massive proportions predominated. A new orderliness emerged.

Actually, the origins of the Bauhaus style could be traced back almost to the beginning of the century. Reacting against the mistiness of the impressionists and the hard-edged realism of Van Gogh and Gauguin, Picasso had begun to work in a style which sought to distill from natural objects certain geometric relationships. The figures in his paintings were outlined in geometric shapes—circles, rectangles, and cubes—and his style became known as cubism.

The new style resembled impressionism only in its retention of the flat plane, the lack of perspective. In Picasso's work, as in the earlier canvases of Braque and in some by Matisse, surfaces are related somewhat like those of a

261

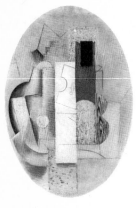

*C*ubist method of creating a geometrical system out of subject matter, or of imposing one on the subject, can be seen in four paintings with musical themes: Braque's *Musical Forms* (left), and (opposite) Picasso's simple study of a violin (top), his small study of a violin and guitar, and his complex *Man With Violin.*

prism, held together in a formal discipline and balanced subtly one against the other. Picasso seldom abandoned the object, concerning himself with portraits and still-life objects. The Dutch Piet Mondrian and others, however, extended the process of abstraction to the point of absolute geometrical simplicity.

Thus, the trend toward formalism appeared to represent the ultimate destiny of the expressionists. In Germany itself, Kandinsky's works from 1920 on assumed more rigid aspect. The former broad and rough splashes of color now were enclosed within geometric patterns. And Paul Klee worked with great zest and wit to create designs out of sharp, clean lines that often resembled a kind of idealized calligraphy.

In 1922, the year of James Joyce's *Ulysses* and T. S. Eliot's *The Waste*

Land, Arnold Schoenberg published his *Method of Composing with Twelve Tones,* the essay which was to be the cornerstone of a new musical revolution. It was not a revolution for Schoenberg himself, or for his disciples; it was the systematic formulation of a style toward which they had tended for well over a decade. The traditional institution of tonality as the basis of musical composition, challenged by Wagner, vestigial in the works of Mahler, could now be officially replaced by a new tradition, that of *atonality.*

Schoenberg's thesis was that each of the twelve notes of the Western scale should be of equal importance, because if any one tone predominates it becomes a tonal center in the listener's ear. In twelve-tone composition the composer, Schoenberg said, works with a row of the twelve tones, and must use the notes in the order that they appear in the row, or in specific permutations of that order. Actually, the ways in which this can be done provide for infinite flexibility; notes can be introduced one after the other, for example, or simultaneously in chords. The important thing, however, is that all notes be used as elements of equal importance, in a series both loose and restricting. Thus the concept of *serialism* entered music.

One of the most important aspects of Schoenberg's thesis, one often misunderstood by listeners, is that the tone-row device is a principle devised strictly for the composer's own use. It is not meant to be heard, as are the themes in a Beethoven symphony. It is, in other words, an inner constructive device, somewhat "secret." Here again Schoenberg gives evidence of his affinity to the Gothic spirit; the polyphonic works of Machaut, for example, and of the Netherlands composers of the fifteenth century, are full of constructive secrets.

While the validity of Schoenberg's principles is still widely challenged, the works he and his followers produced in the twelve-tone style at least attest to the variety possible within that style. Such Schoenberg scores as the Fourth String Quartet, the Violin Concerto, and the opera *Moses und Aron,* each of them entirely based on a single row, are cohesive and dramatically valid.

The variety possible within the twelve-tone system is nowhere better demonstrated than by comparing Schoenberg's two major disciples, Berg and

264

*T*he *Sonata* (right) an early Duchamp work, is crowded with multitude of images, while subject is shunted off to right. Both Leger's *The City* (below) and Mondrian's *Composition* (opposite) use image as departure point, but engulf it in geometrical derivatives.

Webern, both of them Viennese like their teacher. Berg, it may be said, succeeded in effecting a reconciliation between the principles of atonality and romanticism; Webern applied the principles almost entirely to classicism. Or, to put it another way, Berg came to represent the musical counterpart of representational expressionism, while Webern served as the exponent of the non-representational side.

In his opera *Wozzeck*, Berg works with a style founded largely on Mahler's tortured chromaticism, onto which such expressionistic devices as Schoenbergian speech-song are sometimes grafted. Pure atonality is used only sporadically, in scenes representing mental derangement. His final completed work, the haunting Violin Concerto, is completely twelve-tone, but the row is so chosen that it suggests several kinds of simple melodies, and at the end of the work it blends into a Bach chorale. The emotional power of Berg's finest scores is as palpable as anything of Wagner, partly because romanticism tempered his approach to the new techniques.

Webern's music almost completely lacks this kind of romantic luxuriance. His scores are incredibly terse; a characteristic movement rarely takes over two minutes to perform. His orchestration is similarly barren, stripped to the essentials, with a melodic line that often is broken up among various instruments so that it emerges in a series of pinpoints. Silence often becomes as important as sound; it is a generative, tense silence in which the last previous sound is supposed to achieve greater expression by being allowed to expand in the consciousness. In these scores the use of the twelve-tone system can be found at its purest; one often senses, in fact, that Webern is applying the concept of serialism to other elements besides the notes themselves—to rhythm, tone color, dynamics. If Berg shares the luxuriant expressionism of the early paintings of Kandinsky, or of such later subjective-symbolic painters as Max Beckmann, then the works of Webern can be likened to the miniatures of Paul Klee.

Taken together, Schoenberg, Berg, and Webern represent the other of the two major pathways taken by music during the first half of the twentieth century, the one whose direction has pointed consistently away from tonality and toward new methods of achieving logical musical organization. In this respect they belong with the painters who made radically new approaches to their art: the expressionists, and the group loosely banded together as cubists. However they may have differed in dealing with form and expression, these painters and composers shared the pathway of innovation.

The second broad way is that of the nationalist schools and those who sought to find new inspiration within the principles of classicism. In working out new ideas, these artists—unlike the innovators—have allowed themselves to be guided by the light of the past.

Both pathways remain open and are still being explored.

13. Exploration

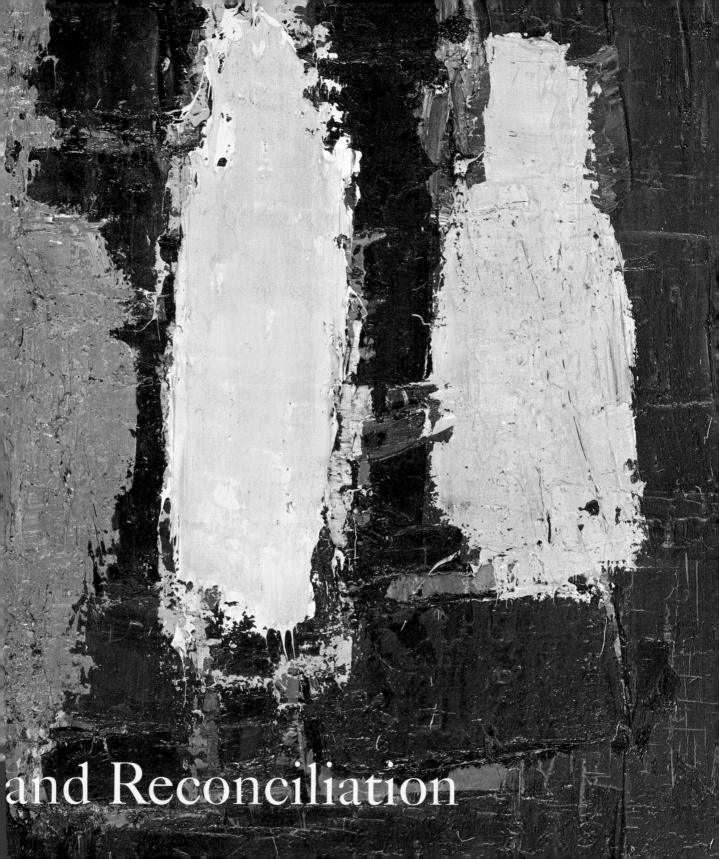

and Reconciliation

Ours is a history-minded civilization. Our cultural past, both recent and distant, is accessible to us as it was to no previous generation. We see the past in perspective, and we are often tempted to place our own era in some sort of perspective as well, as though we could project ourselves into the future and look back. We cannot, but we try.

Technology has had a strange effect on cultural time. Throughout this history of the development of the visual and musical arts, a series of plateaus, usually of considerable duration, has been discerned. Two centuries, more or less, were occupied with the formation of the Renaissance. A century and a half is covered by the baroque era. The spirit of romanticism began to make itself felt around 1750, and did not really recede until the First World War; its vestiges are, in fact, still with us.

The pace of change has quickened. As soon as an era has established itself, it disappears. The artist seems terrified of repeating himself, of becoming known for some particular stylistic trait. To keep up with the times is hardly enough; the artist feels constantly pressed to innovate. And his milieu is crowded with other artists struggling in just the same way.

Nevertheless, the midpoint in the twentieth century was to some degree a time of reconciliation. The two principal pathways pursued by composers in the first half of the century at times converged, with a resultant synthesis of styles that had until then seemed incompatible.

The reconciliations themselves took many forms. In the case of Bela Bartok, for example, the reconciliation took the form of a mellowing toward romantic ideals. Bartok had been known for a style which, although shaped from folk elements, expressed itself in a percussive, astringent manner. In his last two compositions, however—the Third Piano Concerto and the Concerto for Orchestra—he found a way of simplifying his language, drawing from his orchestra tones of warmer coloration, using harmonic resources of less pungency, and creating music that the public found more heartwarming. His Concerto for Orchestra is one of the few large-scale orchestral compositions of the past few decades to have entered the popular orchestral repertory.

For Igor Stravinsky, the reconciliation has taken a somewhat different form. Since the 1920's, Stravinsky had continued to cultivate the hard-edged, clear neoclassic manner of his Octet. The style worked for him in many forms, culminating in the opera *The Rake's Progress*, clearly modeled on the recitative-with-aria format of the late baroque and classical opera, even employing a small, Mozart-sized orchestra with harpsichord. Soon after this opera was launched, Stravinsky began writing in the style to which his music always had stood as the modern antithesis—atonality. In assimilating elements from the atonal language, his model was not so much the large-scale romanticism of Schoenberg and Berg, as the more dry-point manner of Anton von Webern, with its pinpricks of sound and its melody subtly spread among small instrumental groups. Again, Stravinsky made an amalgamation work for him—in such large-scale pieces as his *Threni* for chorus and orchestra, and also in a series of terse, extremely brief chamber compositions.

In recent years, others from the ranks of the so-called conservatives have also experimented with some of the atonalists' ideas: Aaron Copland, in his Fantasy for Piano and the Nonet for Strings, has assimilated the tense organizational scheme propounded by Schoenberg, and has at the same time retained some of his own romantic expansiveness. As was shown early in the atonal era by Alban Berg, atonal techniques can lead in many directions.

Many composers have found that the powerful, tense, mysterious atmosphere created by the atonal language is very much to their liking but have achieved this effect without actually employing Schoenberg's methods. Roger Sessions is such a composer. His music is craggy, deriving its power from sharply clashing dissonances in contrapuntal combinations, atonal in effect but worked out of small melodic elements rather than actual rows. A Sessions pupil, the Californian Andrew Imbrie, has also attracted attention for his work which is similar, although in a style somewhat more romantically oriented than that of his teacher. The Argentinian Alberto Ginastera, whose early works were largely nationalistic-romantic in character, has also joined the nonserial atonalists, and in his opera, *Don Rodrigo*, has created a latter-day

*O*pening pages: By calling his work *Painting*, Nicolas de Staël attests to contemporary artist's frequent desire to assume freedom and to impart it to his audience. So, too, does the picture's implied overlap of media.

273

*O*pposite: Chagall's *Snowing* creates an element both narrative and full of personal mystery. Georgia O'Keeffe's *Deer's Horn Near Cameron* (above) similarly uses familiar imagery in individualistic juxtapositions. Andrew Wyeth's *Spool Bed* (left) also employs folk images, but in a more straightforward way.

275

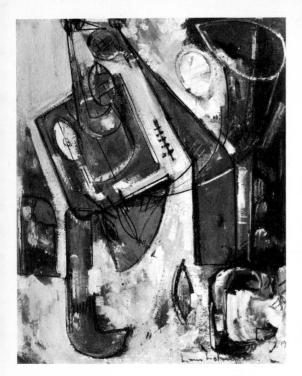

romantic grand opera in totally atonal style. The Italian Luigi Dallapiccola has also achieved a synthesis of atonality and pure lyricism.

The works of these men represent a continuance of the spirit of expressionism in its original implications: strong, personal emotion set forth with intensity of color and without regard for naturalistic outlines. They are united in this sense with a number of painters, notably Hans Hofmann and Franz Kline, whose works also preserve precepts of expressionism.

Other ideals have also persisted, from an even remoter past. The romantic tradition has been reëxamined by a large number of composers throughout the world, and found valid even in our own times. Thus, such Americans as Samuel Barber, William Schuman, and Walter Piston have created broad, oratorical, basically lyrical works in which one senses the shadows of Schumann and Brahms. The German Paul Hindemith, astonishingly facile in all forms during his long and illustrious career, was even more clearly the spiritual descendant of Brahms, not only in his lyrical gifts but also in the strength and logic of his contrapuntal textures.

These men, reactionary as they might be considered, furnished proof that older styles, used with insight, can be kept viable long after they are formed. Within the turbulence of change among today's radicals, the conservatives have established a solid plateau on which they base much of today's new music. They share this plateau with a number of contemporary romantic painters: Georgia O'Keeffe and Andrew Wyeth among the Americans, and the folk-inspired, French-Russian colorist, Marc Chagall.

These, then, are the forces that offer resistance to the flood tide of radicalism that has swept over the arts since 1950. Naturally, the surge had long been gathering, though its tributary elements went largely unheeded for long periods. As long ago as 1925, for example, the French-born American Edgard Varèse had been creating slashing, vibrant studies in startling sound, ranging in volume from that of a solo flute, to that of an ensemble of percussion instruments joined by sirens and wind machines. Even earlier, the Czech Aloys Haba wrote music for strings that used intervals smaller than those of our customary chromatic scale. The music of Webern, carrying the principles of serialism

*H*ans Hofmann's *Delight* (opposite page, left) brings expressionist ideas into present. Calder's mobile *Lobster Trap and Fishtail* uses space as part of the artistic design, an idea expressed musically by Stockhausen and other composers. Pollock's *Autumn Rhythm*, purposely created with great speed and little attempt at control, mirrors "chance" compositions of composers like John Cage.

277

seemingly to their outer limit, went largely ignored except by a small group of intellectuals. So, by and large, were the experiments of Ives and Ruggles.

Suddenly the experiments of these men bore fruit. Under the supervision of Herbert Eimert and Karlheinz Stockhausen, the Cologne studios of the German Radio built a laboratory for the production of sounds by electronic means, manipulating them on recording tape to produce an incredible new sound spectrum totally independent from the symphony orchestra. From these sounds could come melodic and harmonic elements even beyond the imagination of men like Varèse and Haba, and sound combinations even more daring than those of Ives and Ruggles.

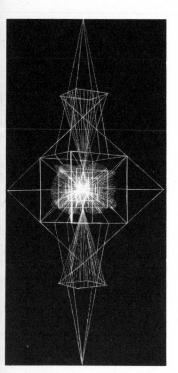

This came about at the same time that the music of Webern suddenly was finding its audience. And the combination of these events suggested to a large group of young composers vast new horizons in musical control—control not over pitches, as suggested by the twelve-tone system, but also over timbre, rhythm, all the elements of a composition. Webern also served as inspiration because of his remarkably clean, delicate range of sounds, and because his very use of silence had an almost spiritual implication.

Thus began the "Age of Webern," and, with it, a new kind of composer—the scientific, mathematical, acoustical-minded composer-engineer. Using electronic sounds on tape, alone or combined with instruments, composers like Stockhausen and the American Milton Babbitt have produced music free not only of tonality, but also of the scale itself, and of the inadequacies of human performers. Tape gave the composer control of the music, and even—through the use of multichannel recording—of the space surrounding the music.

Webern's art won adherents, also, among nonelectronic composers: Pierre Boulez in France, Luigi Nono in Italy, and Babbitt in the United States as represented by some of his earlier works. Like the electronic composers, these men also sought a serial technique which, though divorced more than ever before from traditional practices, still allowed the composer to maintain rigid, formal control over the piece. It became music that was totally abstract, concerned with itself as an end in itself.

278

This approach, known as formal abstractionism, had its counterpart in the visual arts, in the dominant concern for compositional or spatial elements found in the art of, say, Alexander Calder and Jacques Lipchitz. Lipchitz's three-dimensional shapes are anchored; Calder's usually hang freely, moved by motors or by the passing breeze. The works of both are abstract, rigidly conceived, prevailingly constructivist in their outlook.

But a Calder mobile is not immutably structured by its creator; it is subject to the whim of the particular currents of air that turn its constituent parts one way or another. Jackson Pollock, in creating his strange dizzying canvases by dripping paint onto them, introduced the element of accident into the final product. Thus the work of these men is subject, to some degree, to the element of chance.

As might be expected, the same element found its way into music. Instead of writing in such a manner as to retain creative control over their work, certain composers have chosen to give control either partially or entirely to the performer.

In the typical chance compositions by Karlheinz Stockhausen, John Cage, or Earle Brown, the elements out of which the piece is built are given as fragments on the printed page. The performer must in some way make his own choices among these elements, deciding in which order they are to appear, or deciding the actual pitches to go with a given rhythm or sonority. Chance music, in some ways, rekindles the improvisatory element that was found in some of the virtuosic music for strings or voice in the late baroque. But here are differences because, again, the sense of harmony is suspended, and the language is more likely to be that of a latter-day Webern than Scarlatti.

On the one hand, then, we have a music that is more rigidly controlled by formula than ever before: on the other, a music that is totally unpredictable, subject to the whim of the performer. Is there nothing in between, no area of exploration by the avant-garde that resembles the formal principles of the past?

Yes and no. One avenue of exploration suggests itself in the continuing interplay between popular and serious musical styles. From certain elements

Curious mirroring exists between delicate, wiry lines of Richard Lippold's Variation #7, Full Moon, *and page from electronic music score by Stockhausen. Like many medieval music manuscripts, Stockhausen's "notations" are almost as much art as music.*

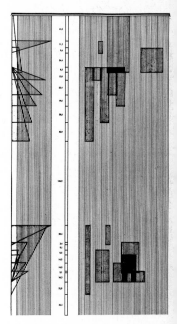

in popular music, notably from jazz, composers have found inspiration for concert music. Gunther Schuller and Larry Austin have created large-scale concert pieces in the serial idiom into which jazz elements have been worked. The results have, at least, been smoother and far less self-conscious than the attempts by Gershwin three decades earlier. Just as elements from the popular, or nonartistic, world have found their way into art museums as Pop Art and Op Art, so does the cross-feeding flourish in the musical world.

But this is only one possibility. If the previous history of the arts can be taken as a valid indication, it is safe to assume that from the various avenues of experimentation being followed today, some sort of synthesis will take place. Part of the fascination in observing the mainstreams of artistic development is the realization that the exact nature of that synthesis, that reconciliation, is impossible to predict. Perhaps it will not occur. Thirty years ago, however, it would have been absurd to suggest that there would some day be a rapprochement between the ideals of Stravinsky and Webern. Yet that has happened.

The listener is caught in the middle, of course, as he always is. In 1912 an Austrian critic refused to review Schoenberg's *Pierrot Lunaire*, claiming that since he was a music critic and the composer had not written any music, he saw no need to write any words. Today's listener finds *Pierrot Lunaire* a comfortable-sounding echo of the now-familiar style of Gustav Mahler.

But the very fact of cross-feeding among the arts—which has been traced through these pages for a period of over two thousand years—should at least suggest a way out of the dilemma. The listener who feels out of touch with some of today's musical developments can, beyond any question, enhance his understanding of this music by observing contemporary developments in painting, sculpture, and architecture.

For the separate arts do not exist in isolation. Together they provide a key to the prevailing creative impulses of their time: a firsthand report, worded directly from the inner consciousness of the creators themselves. Together they form a body which draws upon the spirit of the time, each in its own way. Together they attest strongly to the integrity of the whole of artistic creation.

*B*ridget Riley's Op Art creation, *Current*, involves eye of viewer in reacting to the fluid, changing shape of her work. Today's performer of avant-garde music is similarly impelled to choice by the fluid, changing nature of many of these compositions.

281

Picture Credits

CHAPTER 7
136-137: ARB, Musée Jacquemart-Andre, Paris.
140: Copyright reserved. 142, 143: Giraudon. 144:
ARB, Marburg. 147: Tony Angermayer, Photo
Researchers.

CHAPTER 8
150-151: The Frick Collection. 153: The Sterling
and Francine Clark Art Institute, Williamstown,
Massachusetts. 154: MM, Munsey Fund. 155: MM,
Crosby Brown Collection. 157: MM, Bequest of
William K. Vanderbilt. 158: MM, Gwynne M.
Andrews Fund. 159: MM, Crosby Brown
Collection. 161: Hofburg, Vienna. 162: ARB,
Marburg. 163 (top): MM, Gift of Frank Sturgis;
(bottom): MM, Bequest of John L. Cadwalader.
164: NGA. 166: ARB. 169: MM, Rogers Fund.
171: MM, Crosby Brown Collection.

CHAPTER 9
172-173: ARB, Anderson. 177: ARB, Bayerisches
Nationalmuseum, Munich. 178 (left): MM,
Bequest of Collis P. Huntington; (right):
Cincinnati Art Museum. 181: NGA, Gift of W. G.
Russell Allen. 183: Museum of Fine Arts, Boston,
Gift of Mrs. George von Lengerke Meyer. 186:
ARB, Bulloz. 187: MM, Wolfe Fund. 188: ARB,
Alinari. 189: Giraudon. 190: Giraudon. 193: Scala,
Museo del Prado. 194-195: ARB, Alinari.

CHAPTER 10
196-197: American Library Color Slide Co. 200:
The Frick Collection. 201: Cabinet des Dessins,
Louvre. 202: Cleveland Art Museum, Mr. & Mrs.
William H. Marlatt Fund. 203: Gallery of Modern
Art, Huntington Hartford Collection. 204: MM.
206: The Phillips Collection, Washington. 207:
ARB, Bulloz. 209: Courtesy of the Art Institute of
Chicago. 210: Giraudon. 211: NYPL. 213: Sterling
and Francine Clark Art Institute. 214: MM. 215:

Museum of Fine Arts, Boston, Gift of Quincy
Adams Shaw. 216: MM, Gift of William Church
Osborn. 218: New York Historical Society. 221:
Philadelphia Museum of Art, Mr. & Mrs. Carroll
S. Tyson Collection. 222: NYPL. 223: MM, Gift
of Mrs. Henry McSweeney. 224: NGA. 226:
Pierre Berger, Photo Researchers.

CHAPTER 11
228-229: Worcester Art Museum. 235: Corcoran
Gallery of Art, Washington, D.C. 236-237:
Whitney Museum of American Art. 238: NYPL,
Astor, Lenox and Tilden Foundation. 239: MMA.
242 (left): MM, Gift of Mrs. H. O. Havemeyer;
(right): Museum of Fine Arts, Boston. 244: MM,
H. O. Havemeyer Collection. 245: Copyright 1969
by The Barnes Foundation. 246: Princeton
University Library. 247: NYPL. 249: The Solomon
R. Guggenheim Museum. 251: Musée d'Art
Moderne de la Ville de Paris, Time, Inc.

CHAPTER 12
252-253: MMA. 256: NGA, Rosenwald Collection.
257: MMA. 259: Worcester Art Museum. 261:
The Solomon R. Guggenheim Museum. 262, 263
(all): Philadelphia Museum of Art, Louise and
Walter Arensberg Collection. 264: The Yale
University Gallery, Gift of the Societé Anonyme.
265: ARB, Marburg. 266 (top): Philadelphia
Museum of Art, Arensberg Collection; (bottom):
Philadelphia Museum of Art, A. E. Gallatin
Collection. 267, 268: The Solomon R.
Guggenheim Museum.

CHAPTER 13
270-271: MMA, Photo by Malcolm Varon. 274:
City Art Museum of Saint Louis. 275 (top):
MM, Alfred Stieglitz Collection; (bottom):
Whitney Museum of American Art. 276 (left):
MMA; (right): MMA, George A. Hearn Fund.
278: MMA. 279: NYPL. 280: MMA.

Index

Caption references in italics

Abstractionism, formal, 278-79
Africaine, L' (Meyerbeer), 220
Aida (Verdi), 219, *254*
Albinoni, 131
Alexander Nevsky (Prokofiev), 241
Ambrose, Bishop, 26
Amiens Cathedral, *42*, 43, *48*
Ancient world, music of, 14-22
Angelico, Fra, 82-84, *83*, 95
d'Arezzo, Guido, 47
Aristotle, 14-15
Ars Nova, 55-57
Art Nouveau, 247-48
Atonality, 264-68, 273-76
Augustine of Hippo, Saint, 23-25
Austin, Larry, 281
Avant-garde, 9-10

Babbitt, Milton, 278
Bach, Carl Philipp Emanuel, 170, 175
Bach, Johann Christian, 175
Bach, Johann Sebastian, 77, 144-53,
  164, 170-75, 177-79, 191, 208,
  233, 269
  B minor Mass, 149
  Brandenburg Concertos, 148
  Cantata No. 8, 149
  Cantata No. 146, 149
  *Capriccio on the Departure of a
    Beloved Brother*, 144
  Gloria of the Mass, 149
  Passion Oratorio According to
    Matthew, 148-49
  Wachet auf, 149
Barber, Samuel, 276
Barbizon School, 206
Baroque style, 106-49
  architecture, *146*
Bartered Bride, The (Smetana), 214
Bartok, Bela, 241, 250, 272
Bartolomeo, Fra, *84*
Baudelaire, Charles, 246
Bauhaus, 11, 261-63, *264*

Bayeux tapestry, *39*, 45
Beardsley, Aubrey, *247*
Beckmann, Max, 269
Beethoven, Ludwig van, 11, 149,
  165-67, 174, 185-92, 195, 198,
  209, 225, 230, 241, 250, *255*
  Eroica Symphony, 165-67, 185-91,
    198, 225, 230, 250
  Fidelio, 185
  Fifth Symphony, 185, 191, 198-99
  Ninth Symphony, 225, 230
  Opus 70, No. 1, 191
  Pastoral Symphony, 198
  Sixth Symphony, 191-92
  Third Symphony, 165-67, 185-91,
    198, 225, 230, 250
Beggar's Opera, (Gay & Pepusch),
  156, 175
Bellini, Vincenzo, 218-19, 231
Benton, Thomas Hart, 240
Berg, Alban, 260, 264-69, 273
Berlioz, Hector, 199-205, 212,
  220, 227
  Symphonie Fantastique, 199-202
  Grande Messe des Morts, 202-5
  L'Enfance du Christ, 205
  Les Troyens, 220
Bernini, Giovanni, 107, 109, 114, 124
Biber, Heinrich, 144
Biblical Sonatas (Kuhnau), 144
Binchois, Gilles, 64
Bizet, Georges, 220
Blake, William, 180, *180*
Blaue Reiter, der, 258-61
Bloch, Ernest, 22
B minor Mass (Bach, J. S.), 149
Bonnard, Pierre, 248
Borghese, Pauline, 163
Boris Godunov, (Mussorgsky),
  231, 234
Borodin, Alexander, 231
Bosch, Hieronymus, 70, 71, 138, 257
Botticelli, Sandro, *81*, 88, *90*, 95

Boucher, François, 153, *156*
Boulez, Pierre, 278
Brahms, Johannes, 27, 208-9,
  214-17, 230, 234, 241, 276
Brandenburg Concertos
  (Bach, J. S.), 148
Braque, Georges, 258, 261-63, *263*
Britten, Benjamin, 234
Brown, Earle, 279
Bruckner, Anton, 254-55
Brueghel, Pieter, 70, 72, 138
Brunelleschi, Filippo, 73
Burgundian Court, 63-65
Burne-Jones, Sir Edward, *203*, 208
Buxtehude, Dietrich, 141
Byrd, William, 102, 123, 234
Byzantine, pre-iconoclastic, *28*
Byzantium, 22-31

Caccia, 57
Caccini, Giulio, 110
Cage, John, 10, 279
Calder, Alexander, 277, 279
Calvin, John, 80-81
Camerata, 107-11
Canaletto, Antonio, 135
Canon, 52
Canova, Antonio, 163, *175*
Cantata, 139-41
Canzona, 127-28
Capriccio, 127
*Capriccio on the Departure of a
  Beloved Brother* (Bach, J. S.), 144
Caravaggio, Michelangelo Merisi da,
  100, 107, *109*, 146
Carmen (Bizet), 220
Carolingian art, *30*
Castiglione, *127*
Carpeaux, Jean Baptiste, *214*
Cavalleria Rusticana (Mascagni),
  243
Cellini, Benvenuto, *87*
Cézanne, Paul, *244*

Chace, 57
Chaconne, 127
Chagall, Marc, *275, 277*
Chamber music, 170-71
Chance music, 279
Chanson, 90
Charpentier, Gustave, 246
Charpentier, Marc Antoine, 123
Chartres, Cathedral of, *37*
Chausson, Ernest, 245
Chavez, Carlos, 240
Cherubini, Luigi, 184, 217, 220
Chopin, Frédéric, 206, 209, 217-18, 246
Chorale, 80-81
Chorale-prelude, 141
Christianity, music of, 22-57
Chromatic Fantasia (Sweelinck), 141
Cimabue, Giovanni, 60-61, *62*
Cimarosa, Domenico, 175, 217
Classical Symphony (Prokofiev), 11
Classicism, decline of, 174-95
C major Fantasy *(Wanderer)* (Schubert), 192, 195, 199
Cocteau, Jean, 248
Colored Leaves (Schumann), 205
Concerto, 167
Concerto grosso, 128
Conductus, 51
Conservatism and nationalism, 233-34
Constable, John, 206-8
Constantine, Emperor, 25
Copland, Aaron, 237-38, 273
Copley, John Singleton, 180, *182*
Corelli, Arcangelo, 127-31, 143, 168, 177, 191
Corinth, Lovis, *255-57*
Coronation of Poppaea, The (Monteverdi), 120
Corot, Camille, *201, 205,* 206, 244
Così fan Tutte (Mozart, W. A.), 179

Counterpoint, 35-45, 139
Couperin, François, 153-55, 248
Courbet, Gustave, 212, *212*
Creation (Haydn), 179, 225
Cristofori pianoforte, *171*
Cubism, 261-63
Cycladic sculpture, *17*

Dance music, 90-95
Dante Alighieri, 61, 96
Das Lied von der Erde (Mahler), 255
Daumier, Honoré, *211,* 212
David, Jacques Louis, 181-84, *186,* 244
Debussy, Claude, 246-48
Degas, Edgar, 246
Delacroix, Eugène, 184, *189, 199, 206,* 244
Della Robbia, *75*
Devin du Village, Le (Rousseau), 159
Dido and Aeneas (Purcell), 123
Dissonance, 101-2
Distortion, musical and pictorial, 95-102
Donatello, 73, *75*
Don Carlo (Verdi), 219
Don Giovanni (Mozart), 179
Donizetti, Gaetano, 218-19
Dowland, John, 101-2
Duccio of Siena, 60-61, *62*
Duchamp, Marcel, *266*
Dufay, Guillaume, 64-68, 72
Dunstable, John, 64-66
Duomo of Florence, 73, *75*
Dürer, Albrecht, 75-76, 77, 81, 138
Dvorak, Antonin, 212-14, 230, 240
Dying Niobid, 16

Eakins, Thomas, *234,* 239
Eimert, Herbert, 278
Electronic music, 278

Elgar, Sir Edward, 234
Elijah (Mendelssohn), 208
Enfance du Christ, L' (Berlioz), 205
Erkel, Ferenc, 233
Erlach, Fischer von, 146-48
Eroica Symphony (Beethoven), 165-67, 185-91, 198, 225, 230, 250
Ethics, music and, 14-15
Ethos, Greek music and, 15-16
Euridice (Caccini & Peri), 110
Expressionism, 257-69

Falla, Manuel de, 240
Falstaff, (Verdi), 219-20, 243
Fantasia, 127
Fantasia on a Theme by Tallis (Vaughan Williams), 27, 234
Fauré, Gabriel, 246-47
Faust (Liszt), 205
Fidelio (Beethoven), 185
Fingal's Cave (Mendelssohn), 208
Five, The, 231-32, 240-41
Five Pieces for Orchestra (Schoenberg), 260
Flying Dutchman, The, (Wagner), 223
Fontainebleau School, 90
Four Seasons, The, (Vivaldi), 131-34
Fragonard, Jean Honoré, 153, *153*
Francesca, Piero della, *83,* 84, 87
Franck, César, 244-45
Freischütz, Der (Weber), 211-12, 217
Frescobaldi, Girolamo, 114, 141
Fugue, 141-43
Fuseli, John Henry, 163, *167*

Gabrieli, Andrea, 87
Gabrieli, Giovanni, 87
Gainsborough, Thomas, *178,* 180
Galilei, Vincentio, 107
Gauguin, Paul, 257, *258,* 261

Gay, John, 156, 175
Geminiani, Francesco, 131
Gershwin, George, 237, 281
Gesualdo, Don Carlo, 101
Ginastera, Alberto, 273-76
Giotto di Bondone, 61-63, *62*, 82
Gluck, Christoph, 159-60, *160*, 164,
   175, 220
Goes, Hugo van der, 70-71
Goethe, Johann Wolfgang von,
   163, 192, 211
Gothic style, 45-52
Goudimel, Claude, 81
Gounod, Charles, 220, 244
Goya, Francisco, 184, *192*, *195*, 220
Granados, Enrique, 240
Grande Messe des Morts (Berlioz),
   202-5
Greco, El, *98*, 100-1, 106
Greece, ancient, 14-19
   artifacts, *19*
Gregorian chant, 26-31, 48
Grieg, Edvard, 212, 230, 234
Gropius, Walter, 261
Grosz, George, 258
Grünewald, Mathias, *98*, 101, 138
Guarini, Guarino, 128-30

Haba, Aloys, 277-78
Halka (Moniuszko), 233
Handel, George Frederick, 134-38,
   152, 179, 233
Harmony, 165
Harpsichords, *155*, *159*
Harris, Roy, 237
Haydn, Joseph, 135, 174, 176-80,
   185, 191, 195
Haydn, Michael, 175
Hebrew music, 19-22
Heilige deutsche Kunst (Wagner),
   254
Henry VIII, 80

Hindemith, Paul, 276
Hoffmann, E. T. A., 184
Hofmann, Hans, 276, 277
Hogarth, William, *164*, 180
Holy Shroud, Chapel, 130, *131*
Homer, Winslow, 239
Honegger, Arthur, 248
Houdon, Jean Antoine, 163
Huguenots, Les (Meyerbeer), 220
Humanism, 60-61

Imbrie, Andrew, 273
Impressionism, 246-48
Indian music, 15
d'Indy, Vincent, 245
Ingres, Jean Auguste, *191*, *206*, *209*
Instrumental music
   baroque, 114, 127-35, 141-44
   Renaissance, 102-3
   Romantic, 153-56, 164-71
Isorhythm, 56
Ives, Charles, 238-39, 278

Janacek, Leos, 240
Jannequin, Clément, 90
Josquin des Prés, 76-77, 81, 84
Joyce, James, 263
Jupiter Symphony (Mozart), 177

Kandinsky, Wassily, 9, 258-60, *260*,
   263, 269
Key, musical, 65
Kirchner, Ernst, 257
Klee, Paul, 263, *268*, 269
Kline, Franz, 276
Kodaly, Zoltan, 241
Kokoschka, Oskar, 9, 258
Kuhnau, Johann, 144

Lalande, Michel de, 123
Landino, Francesco, 61-63
Laocoön, 16, *25*
Lasso, Orlando di, 101

Le Jeune, Claude, 81
Léger, Fernand, *266*
Leonardo da Vinci, 73-75, *75*, 82
Leoninus, 48
Lessing, Gotthold, 163
Le Sueur, François, 184
Life for the Czar, A (Glinka), 231
Lipchitz, Jacques, *264*, 279
Liszt, Franz, 199-205, 214-17, 227,
   234, 241, 245
Locatelli, Pietro Antonio, 131
Lohengrin (Wagner), 223
Lorenzetti, Ambrogio, 61
Lorrain, Claude, *116*, 121
Louis XIV, 121-23, 144
Love for Three Oranges
   (Prokofiev), 241
Lucia di Lammermoor (Donizetti),
   218-19
Lully, Jean Baptiste, 120-23, *122*
Luther, Martin, 80-81, 139

MacDowell, Edward, 236
Machaut, Guillaume de, 55-57,
   63-64, 257, 264
Madrigal, 96-101
Magic Flute, The (Mozart), 179
Mahler, Gustav, 255-57, 264, 268, 281
Manesse manuscript, *42*
Manet, Edouard, *218*, 220, 227, 246
Manfredini, 131
Mannheim style, 167
Mantegna, *84*
Marc, Franz, 258
Marcello, 131
Markham, Edwin, 212
Marriage of Figaro, The (Mozart),
   179
Marsh, Reginald, *239*, 240
Masaecio, Lorenzo, 61, *62*
Mascagni, Pietro, 243
Mass, 66
Massenet, Jules, 246

Matisse, Henri, *245*, 248, 261-63
Medici, Lorenzo de, 76
Meistersinger von Nürnberg, Die,
    (Wagner), 227, 254
Memling, Hans, *68*, 70
Mendelssohn, Felix, 135, 208, 217
Menotti, Gian Carlo, 243
Messiah, (Handel) 134-35
Meyerbeer, Giacomo, 220, 223, 231,
    234, 244
Michelangelo Buonarroti, 11, *95*,
    95-96, 106-7, 114, 124, 174
Milhaud, Darius, 248
Millet, Jean François, 212, *214*
Mixed media, 9-10
Mondrian, Piet, 263, *266*
Monet, Claude, *231*, 246, *255*
Moniuszko, Stanislaw, 233
Monteverdi, Claudio, 10, 77, 111-13,
    120, 124, 174, 191, 220
Morley, Thomas, 100, 234
Motet, 48-51
Mozart, Wolfgang Amadeus, 8-9,
    11, 77, 149, 174-80, 185, 191-92,
    195, 198, 206, 209, 217, 219, 250
Munch, Edvard, *256*, 258
Music, origin of, 14-31
Mussorgsky, Modest, 231-33

Nationalism, 211-14, 230-46
Naturalism, 81-84, 106-7
Neoclassicism, 248-50
Neuschwanstein, *227*
Nolde, Emil, 257, *257*
Nono, Luigi, 278
Northern style, 63-72
    and Southern style, fusion with,
        73-77

Obrecht, Jacob, 72, 76, 84, 139
Ockeghem, Jan, 72, 76, 84
Octet for Winds (Stravinsky), 250
Offenbach, Jacques, 220-23, 246

O'Keeffe, Georgia, *275*, 277
Opera
    baroque, 107-27, 134-41, 144
    origins of, 110-20
    Romantic, 156-60, 163-64, 217-27
Oratorio, 114-17
Orchestra, development of, 164-70
Orfeo L' (Monteverdi), 111-13, 124
Organum, 43-45
Orozco, José, *239*, 240
Orpheus (Gluck), 164
Orpheus in Hades (Offenbach), 220
Ossian, 184
Otello (Verdi), 219, 243

Paganini, Niccolo, 199-202
Paine, John Knowles, 236
Paisiello, Giovanni, 175
Palestrina, Giovanni da, 88, 114
Panini, G. B., *143*, *159*
Panthéon (Paris), 160, *163*
Parsifal (Wagner), 227, *255*
Parthenon, 16, *23*
Passacaglia, 127
Pathos, Greek music and, 16
Paul (Saint), 22
Pelléas et Mélisande (Debussy), 247
Pepusch, Christoph, 156, 175
Pergolesi, Giovanni, 159, 175, 217
Peri, Jacopo, 110
Peter Grimes (Britten), 234
Petrarch, Francesco, 61-63, 96
Petrouchka (Stravinsky), 250
Pfitzner, Hans, 255
Pianoforte, 167, *171*, 223
Picasso, Pablo, 248, *250*, 258, 261-63,
    263
Pierrot Lunaire (Schoenberg), 281
Piston, Walter, 276
Plato, 14-16
Pollock, Jackson, 277, 279
Porgy and Bess (Gershwin), 237
Poulenc, Francis, 248

Poussin, Nicolas, *110*, *115*, 121
Pozzo, Fra Andrea, *134*
Prelude to the Afternoon of a Faun,
    (Debussy), 247
Prokofiev, Serge, 11, 241
Prometheus (Scriabin), 260
Puccini, Giacomo, 243
Purcell, Henry, 123, 134
Pythagoras, 15, 39

Quantz, Johann, 175
Queen Mary's Psalter, *56*

Raga, 15
Rake's Progress, The (Stravinsky),
    273
Rameau, Jean Philippe, 153-56, 248
Raphael, 88, *88*, 95, 121
Ravel, Maurice, 248
Ravenna mosaic, *29*
Realism, 211-14
Reger, Max, 255
Rembrandt, *139*, *145*, 146
Renaissance, 60-103
Reni, Guido, *113*, 120, 130
Renoir, Auguste, *242*, 246, *255*
Repin, Ilya, 231, *232*
Requiem (Mozart), 179-80
Reynolds, Sir Joshua, *178*
Rhenish Symphony (Schumann),
    205-6
Ricercare, 127, 141
Rienzi (Wagner), 223
Rigoletto (Verdi), 219
Riley, Bridget, *281*
Rimsky-Korsakov, Nikolai, 231,
    234, 240
Ring of the Nibelungen, The
    (Wagner), 227
Rite of Spring, The (Stravinsky),
    250
Ritornello, 170

Rivera, Diego, 240
Rococo, 153-56, 160
Romanesque period, 34-45, *37*
Romanticism, 198-227
  rise of, 152-71
Rondo, 170
Rossini, Gioacchino, 218
Rousseau, Henri, 248, *248*
Rousseau, Jean Jacques, 159, 163
Rubens, Peter Paul, 138, *143*
Rude, François, *201, 205*
Ruggles, Carl, 238-39, 278
Ryder, Albert Pinkham, *225*

Saint-Saëns, Camille, 246
Saint Mark's Cathedral (Venice), *87*
Saint Peter's Basilica, *107*, 114, *124*
Sassetta, 61
Satie, Erik, 248
Scarlatti, Alessandro, 126-27, 131
Scarlatti, Domenico, 131, 168, 279
Schelomo (Bloch), 22
Schiller, Johann von, 163, 192
Schoenberg, Arnold, 9, 56, 258-60,
  264-69, 273
Schubert, Franz, 174, 192-95, 199,
  211, 217, 247, 255
Schuller, Gunther, 281
Schuman, William, 276
Schumann, Robert, 205-9, 217, 255,
  230, 245, 276
Schütz, Heinrich, 120, 138-41
Scottish Symphony
  (Mendelssohn), 208
Scriabin, Alexander, 260
Seasons, The (Haydn), 179, 198
Serialism, 264
Serva Padrona, La (Pergolesi),
  159, 175
Seurat, Georges, *4*
Shakespeare, William, 100
Shostakovich, Dimitri, 241
Sibelius, Jan, 233

Sidney, Sir Philip, 100
Singspiel, 175
Six, The, 248
Smetana, Bedrich, 212-14, 230, 240
Soldier's Tale, The (Stravinsky), 250
Solomon (Handel), 134
Sonata, 128
Soufflot, Jacques, 160
Southern style, 73-77
Spring Symphony (Schumann) 206
Staël, Nicolas de, *273*
Stamitz, Johann, 167
Stockhausen, Karlheinz, 278-79, *279*
Stradivari, Antonio, 127
Strauss, Johann, II, 212
Strauss, Richard, 254-55
Stravinsky, Igor, 11, 240-41, 248-50,
  273, 281
Suite, 143-44
Surprise Symphony (Haydn), 165
Surikov, Vassily, 231
Sweelinck, Jan, 141
Symphonic poem, 199
Symphony, 167-70

Tales of Hoffmann (Offenbach), 223
Tannhäuser (Wagner), 223
Tchaikovsky, Peter, 232-33, 238, 241
Telemann, Georg Philipp, 134
Theodor, Carl, 167
Thomas, Ambroise, 220
Thomson, Virgil, 238
Threni (Stravinsky), 273
Tiepolo, Giovanni, *128*, 128-30
Tintoretto, 87-88, *95*, 96, 100, 106
Titian, 87, 96, *96*
Toccata, 103, 127
Tonality, 9, *65*
Traviata, La (Verdi), 219
Trio sonata, 128
Tristan und Isolde (Wagner),
  227-30, 247, 255, 260
Trovatore, Il (Verdi), 219

Troyens, Les (Berlioz), 220
Turner, William, *203*, 208

Uccello, Paolo, 84, 87, 95
Unfinished Symphony (Schubert),
  195

Van der Weyden, Rogier, *68*
Van Eyck, Hubert, 64-68, 82
Van Eyck, Jan, 64-68, *66*, 82
Van Gogh, Vincent, *255*, 255-57, 261
Varèse, Edgard, 277-78
Vaughan Williams, Ralph, 27, 234
Verdi, Giuseppe, 77, 212, 218-20,
  234, 243-44, 254
Vermeer, Jan, *9*, *141*, 146
Versailles, *120*, 123
Victoria, Tomás Luis de, 101
Villa-Lobos, Heitor, 240
Virginal, *103*
Vitry, Philippe de, 55
Vivaldi, Antonio, 131-34, 152

Wagner, Richard, 10, 101, 194, 198,
  217, 223-230, 254-55, 260, 264, 269
Walton, William, 234
Wanderer Fantasy (Schubert), 192,
  195, 199
Watteau, Antoine, 153, *153, 155*
Weber, Carl Maria von, 211-12, 217
Webern, Anton von, 260, 264-69,
  273, 277-81
Weckmann, Mathias, 141
Wedding, The (Stravinsky), 250
Weyden, Rogiér van der, 68-70
Wilbye, John, 100
Willaert, Adrian, 87
William Tell (Rossini), 218
Wood, Grant, *236*, 240
Worringer, Wilhelm, 257
Wozzeck (Berg), 268
Wren, Sir Christopher, 135, 146, 160
Wyeth, Andrew, *275*, 277